Martha,

May God bless

Dr Anthony J

SHAME
IDENTITY THIEF

JOHN E BENNETT
55 FARREL ST
ROUNDUP MT 59072-6904

Endorsements

The most important understanding that we can have in the time that we are presently living is who we are. Your identity is you expressing who you were made to be. Just as many individuals have experienced identity theft in the natural, we must remember that the enemy comes to steal, kill and destroy. Satan has a strategy to remove the identity and expression of who we are in Christ. Henry Malone's book, *Shame: Identity Thief*, is excellent. The enemy does not play fair with our traumas or failures. He has a strategy to create a failure mentality within us. This book helps you remove a "sticky" covering of shame linked with your past. This is also a wonderful book to assist you in finding out who you were meant to be. I highly recommend *Shame: Identity Thief* for those who are searching for significance.

Chuck D. Pierce
President, Glory of Zion International Ministries
Denton, Texas

Why do we humans feel so guilty? Because we are guilty. Sin has consequences and one of its most debilitating aftereffects is shame. Many today try to assuage shame by condoning sin. Like all unscriptural formulas, it just doesn't work. In this important book Henry Malone challenges us to come to grips with our sins, make a full repentance and leave them at the liberating cross of Jesus Christ. He bore all our sin and its accompanying shame. Amazingly the antidote to pride on the one hand and a poor self image on the other is the same—to know who you are in Christ. *Shame: Identity Thief* will point you to lasting liberty.

> **David Shibley**
> *President, Global Advance*
> *Dallas, Texas*

Shame: Identity Thief is a book full of powerful revelation, Biblical insights and knowledge. Henry Malone shares his personal journey of overcoming the pain of shame. This book touches the depths of the soul and will be a great help to everyone who has experienced personal shame. This is a deliverance book for every ministry and individual. I recommend everyone read this book!

> **Apostle John P. Kelly**
> *CEO, LEAD (Leadership Education for Apostolic Development)*
> *CEO, ICWBF (Int'l Christian Wealth Builders Foundation)*

Henry Malone has been my friend for 20 years and I'm very excited about this new book. I'm grateful that someone has finally exposed the SHAME BASED LIFE that so many people have lived since childhood. Thousands of people have discovered new freedom through Dr. Malone's ministry. Now thousands more will experience new freedom through this book. I believe this one book will become a major event in many lives.

> **Dale Gentry**
> *Breakout Prayer Network*
> *Fort Worth, Texas*

Far too many believers have been tormented by feelings of failure and unworthiness, when Jesus died to give them abundant life. But finally, a book has been written exposing the hidden emotion of shame, which is the root of those feelings. The truths contained in this book will change your life. I believe this book should be mandatory reading for all believers because it will save them years of needless pain.

Ken Hansen
Lead Pastor, Living Water Community Church
Bolingbrook, IL

This well-named book is a most thorough treatise on the causes, characteristics and cure of shame, a pandemic among us. A proper identity is an absolute necessity not only to mental health but to normal productivity. Henry Malone uses pertinent illustrations in a presentation laced with relevant Scriptures in identifying and dealing with shame as the thief that has stolen many souls. The book reaches its zenith as the author brings us to recognize that, because of what God has said over and over again, the reader, held down and limited by shame can begin again in a liberated life of freedom by believing and declaring the truth which sets us free. Thanks, Henry, for a splendid book!

Jack Taylor
President, Dimensions Ministries
Melbourne, Florida

Shame: Identity Thief is a well written, easy to read, practical book that initially made me think of all the people I knew who should read it. Then I realized I was looking in the mirror. Dr. Jim Wilder calls shame one of the "big six" negative emotions that every child needs to learn to navigate by 18 months of age (along with sadness, anger, fear, disgust and hopeless-despair), and in my experience no descendant of Adam has been able to avoid at least partially basing our identity on shame. Our Lord Jesus Christ was shamed, but shame was never the basis of His identity. For the rest of us, Dr. Malone has provided encouragement and help to recognize and face the issue head on. The book will help you reduce the load of shame you carry and that is a good thing. We live in a shame based culture and the deeply wounded people we at Restoration in Christ minister to very much need this timely and gentle approach. Highly recommended, I am hoping that our ministry, RCM, will be able to carry the book on our website and sell it at our seminars.

Tom R. Hawkins, Ph.D.
Restoration in Christ Ministries
Grottoes, Virginia

"There is 'a toxic poison' that's destroying some of our most important relationships and will ultimately prevent us from reaching our kingdom potential. We must identify, confront and overcome it. My friend Henry Malone identifies this poison and provides us with 'the divine antidote' in this important new book."

Eddie Smith,
who with his wife Alice offer a free 52-week school of prayer
at www.TeachMeToPray.com

This timeless classic is sure to minister to millions! *Shame: Identity Thief* is a must read by everyone who has experienced or is experiencing shame in their lives. In this book, Henry Malone plainly and boldly identifies the various forms of shame and its affects and he clearly presents the solution on how to get set free from the bondage of shame. I strongly recommend everyone to read this book and then share it with others.

Carl Everett
Director, Bethany Cell Church Network
Publisher of Compassion Magazine

Dr. Henry Malone

Foreword by
John Sandford

**VISION
LIFE**
PUBLICATIONS

First Printing, December 2006

Requests for information should be addressed to:
Vision Life Publications, P.O. Box 153691, Irving, Texas 75015
Email: info@visionlife.org
Web site: http://www.visionlife.org

ISBN 978-0-9717065-4-5

Cover and Layout designed by Ed Tuttle
Printed in the United States of America

CONTENTS

ACKNOWLEDGMENTS

To those who encouraged the writing of this book, to all who contributed financially, to many who have touched my life and helped in my journey out of a shame-based existence, I shall forever be grateful.

For my wife Tina, whose love and support for me have been unfailing, and who spent many hours pouring over and editing my manuscript, thank you.

For my assistant, Karen Frederickson, who faithfully typed, transcribed and proofread this manuscript, thank you.

For Ed Tuttle, who designed another outstanding cover and layout for this book, thank you.

For John Loren Sandford, who was an instrument in God's hands, to help me in the recovery of my true identity, and who took time from his busy schedule to write the foreword, thank you.

For Tony Lincoln, who edited the manuscript, thank you.

For Gloria Hart, a dear friend, who proofread this manuscript, thank you.

For each one who took time to read the manuscript and write endorsements, thank you.

FOREWORD

In his book, *Shame: Identity Thief*, Henry Malone makes us aware of the effects of an emotion we too seldom think about – shame – and how it lies behind more character flaws and behaviors than we have realized. He calls us to be unafraid, thus unashamed, to look at ourselves with candid eyes, to see how often and how much shame has placed colored lenses on our eyes, regarding ourselves and others.

He wants us to see that though we have believed that shame met its death on the cross when we first received Jesus as our Lord and Savior (and it truly did) shame has managed to resurrect and slip under our radar to be the thief that robs us of our Christian identity – and thus our joy. Readers may find themselves set free and restored to the blessed Christian identity we have as sons and daughters of our Father, that is, if we will follow through with prayers that do away with shame and return us to unfettered fellowship with Him and each other. The answer in his book is simple - the grace of Jesus in whom is no condemnation and no blame, only love and acceptance for all who call on His name and seek His face.

John Loren Sandford
Co-Founder, Elijah House
Spokane, WA

INTRODUCTION

I was raised in a home where shame was not a stranger. I often heard, "Shame on you!" for behavior that was considered wrong, inappropriate or embarrassing. As I look back over my life, I never realized how much a part of my existence shame had become. There were numerous facets—like the many colors of thread the weaver uses to create cloth. The actions of my life were accented daily with all kinds of disgrace and thus gave my life's fabric the deep, deep stains of shame.

It all seemed so natural to me; I was an easy target. Shame could cycle again and again in my life, and each time I just reached out and embraced it like a friend. What I didn't realize was how it had twisted my thinking and bound me to a set of repetitive thought-patterns. I drank shame like a glass of cold milk, and it seemed to be good because it created feelings of familiarity.

I was raised in what, in those days, was called a "broken home" and never saw my father until I was about five years old. My stepfather was a strong, happy Christian man who worked hard. But I could never receive all he tried to give me, because shame made me feel I was not worthy. Shame had put gray-colored glasses on me so I couldn't see clearly. I believed there was something fundamentally wrong with me, and everyone knew about it. Life then became a task to do, rather than a journey to enjoy. I had bought into the lie. Therefore, when even the smallest mistake was made and shame was heaped upon me by my caregivers, I willingly accepted that I had done wrong because, somehow, I was wrong.

Shame is a mega-problem in the church today but seems to be rarely recognized by the leaders. They have created doctrines to justify it. Mental health providers have given shame many different names and even try to make it sound "normal". It has been embraced and validated in many Christian circles. We have tried all sorts of things to soften its blows, but still we blindly continue down the track. We *want* to face life without dread, free from the abiding sins of shame that drive us. This is an age-old struggle. It did not begin with you and me, and it will not end with us. You may have gone through the cycle over and over again; nevertheless, there is hope for us all.

> I willingly accepted that I had done wrong because, somehow, I **was** wrong.

As you read this book, you will find principles which will give you keys to unlock your "cage" and break free from shame. You will then be able to enjoy the life that Jesus died to give you – life without a mask.

THE BURDEN OF SHAME

CHAPTER ONE

THE CONCEPT OF SHAME

Many people go through life without giving much thought to what shame is or what it does to them and the people around them. It seems easier to ignore than to acknowledge. It is just one of those negative issues we "should" deal with or, more likely, quickly pass over. We may have no actual understanding of its driving force within us.

Let's begin our journey into the reality of the *unreality* of the shame-based life. Webster's dictionary says shame is a "disturbed or painful feeling of guilt, incompetence, indecency or blameworthiness." As a verb, it is "to make ashamed, to cause to feel shame, to dishonor, to disgrace." Let's look at it from a Christian point of view. True shame is what we experience when we sin and are aware of it—that awful feeling of having missed the mark or failed, regret that we have disappointed God and/or other people. In those circumstances, God has allowed shame to come to draw us back to Him. Like Adam in the Garden of Eden, we have two options. We can run and hide or we can acknowledge our sin, repent of it, and ask God to forgive us. Our fellowship is restored.

> If we confess our sins, He is faithful and just to forgive us our sins and to cleanse us from all unrighteousness. (1 John 1:9)

This is the upside of shame. It drives us to God. Jack Frost says, "Only when shame outweighs the pain in a circumstance are we willing to deal with the shame".[1] This is too often the truth in our lives. More than one kind of shame is probably at play. We will call them true shame and false shame. Dr. Grant Mullins defined it this way, "True shame is what we experience when we sin. We did something wrong. We repent and our relationship can be restored."[2]

On the other hand, false shame (also called toxic shame) is a tool of Satan. It is a fear of being found out, being abandoned or rejected, being exposed or exposing others. False shame is the lie we believe about ourselves, the rejection of God's love and forgiveness based on feelings of personal unworthiness. It will keep us from vulnerability and healing. True shame says, "You did wrong", while false shame says, "You *are* wrong." True shame says, "I made a mistake", but false shame says, "I *am* a mistake." The only remedy for true shame is the cross of Jesus Christ and His blood. The remedy for false shame is *not* to give credit to the lies we have believed about who we are. For example, you are not worth anything, no one really wants you, you are not important, you are ugly, you are a mistake, you should never have been born, etc. Shame has been called a "master emotion" because it binds itself to other emotions, especially when they are denied or repressed. In a shame-based family, emotions like sadness, hurt feelings and loneliness are characterized as weak and ineffective.

> True shame is what we experience when we sin and are aware of it.

Barbara came to me for ministry because she could never be truthful about her feelings with her husband. This caused trouble in the family. She told me that when she was a little girl about five or six years old, she had a doll that she greatly loved. One day, a neighbor's child grabbed it from her and savagely tore it apart. Being devastated, she ran home sobbing to her mother and sister and told them the story. Her mother said to her, "Why are you crying and carrying on so much? It's only a doll. You need to grow up. Stop this nonsense right now." Her mother shamed her for feeling grief and pain.

As she grew up, each time she felt grief or emotional pain, she also felt shame. I ministered to her and asked Jesus to heal her of a heart broken over that childhood doll. I then separated the grief and emotional pain. Now she can grieve and not feel ashamed.

There's no such thing as not being affected by emotions. Our soul is one-third mind, one-third will and one-third emotions. You would have to kill one-third of your soul not to be moved by your emotions.

OUR CREATOR'S ORIGINAL DESIGN

Many people, however, have been extremely successful in repressing their emotions. Our Creator has many emotions, and He created us to experience and give expression to them—sadness, joy, anxiety, psychological pain, or even physical expressions like tapping your foot, clapping your hands or snapping your fingers. Emotion has many faces. But shame will cause us to cover them with a mask. We try to become whatever the family needs, so we give up our identity to please others. All the while, our emotions are being repressed deep within us and, sooner or later, will break out and bring shame upon us. This leads to self-rejection, self-hatred, low self-esteem and chronic unhappiness. Shame causes us to be self-focused.[3] This self-focus makes it almost impossible to admit when we are wrong. Shame brings fear – fear of being out of control, of being vulnerable, of being exposed.

> "Therefore we do not lose heart. Even though our outward man is perishing, yet the inward man is being renewed day by day. For our light affliction, which is but for a moment, is working for us a far more exceeding and eternal weight of glory, while we do not look at the things which are seen, but at the things which are not seen. For the things which are seen are temporary, but the things which are not seen are eternal." (2 Corinthians 4:16-18)

This indicates that we will miss God and His power if we stay self-focused and thus see only the immediate, never the eternal. With this self-centered mindset, you can't see what God's plans are for you. Your identity is lost. The real you is hidden behind so many other things. Often we may be labeled prideful or arrogant, but in reality we are hiding our shame. Sometimes the mask looks like independence and self-reliance. We erect barriers to keep others at a distance. We wall off our hearts so they can't touch us; neither can we feel *their* pain. We are afraid to be vulnerable and found out. Yet, because we have deep emotional wounds, it is hard to keep our mask in place. Others may briefly be able to see through it. So we could say that emotional pain pokes holes in our bucket. We are leaky vessels, and this lets others get a distorted view of who we are. Don't let the foundational lies you believe about yourself keep shame attached. We have merged our experiences and our fundamental lies together so that we refuse to believe what God says about us. We just think we are worthless and no good. We hide behind our mask.

Jean had an exceptionally successful pastorate of two churches. But she was ultimately dismissed by the bishop of her denomination because she could not receive criticism—or compliments. I asked her what kind of home she was raised in and what her relationship was with her father. She replied,

> True shame says, "I made a mistake", but false shame says "I **am** a mistake."

"He always told me I was ugly, and he told my sister she was beautiful. I remember my first day of school. Before I left, I looked into the mirror and kept looking until I could see the ugliness my father said I had. This stayed with me all of my life." Jean was a nice-looking woman with a wonderful personality.

She had believed her father's lies. She combined them with her life-experiences until she acted ugly and worthless. Thus she lost her position as pastor and her marriage, as well. She could never be the real person God created her to be. She lived behind a mask.

In order to defeat shame, we must accept the essential truth that we are made in God's image. We are lovely, beautiful, passionate, gifted, desirable and lovable.

> Then God said, "Let Us make man in Our image, according to Our likeness; let them have dominion over the fish of the sea, over the birds of the air, and over the cattle, over all the earth and over every creeping thing that creeps on the earth," So God created man in His own image; in the image of God He created him; male and female He created them. Then God blessed them, and God said to them, "Be fruitful and multiply; fill the earth and subdue it; have dominion over the fish of the sea, over the birds of the air, and over every living thing that moves on the earth." (Genesis 1:26-28)

God formed each of us in His image in our mother's womb.

For You formed my inward parts;
You covered me in my mother's womb.
I will praise You, for I am fearfully and wonderfully made;
Marvelous are Your works,
And that my soul knows very well.
My frame was not hidden from You,
When I was made in secret,
And skillfully wrought in the lowest parts of the earth.
Your eyes saw my substance, being yet unformed.
And in Your book they all were written,
The days fashioned for me,
When as yet there were none of them.
How precious also are Your thoughts to me, O God!
How great is the sum of them! (Psalm 139:13-17)

God made us in His likeness. God is not ugly, stupid, worthless, trashy, no-good or a liar. Thus we are not those things either. I may do some of them, but I *am* none of those things because I am like my Heavenly Father. I just need to *act* like Him. God knows no shame. Don't let the devil steal your identity by getting you to take in false values and untrue beliefs.

God formed a perfect environment for the man He created. Adam did not know shame as he walked with God in the garden.

Then God saw everything that He had made, and indeed it was very good.
So the evening and the morning were the sixth day. (Genesis 1:31)

Understanding that man needed a companion, God made the woman from Adam's rib.

And they were both naked, the man and his wife, and were not ashamed. (Genesis 2:25)

Man, at this time, was walking in total fellowship with God; thus His presence provided covering for them, and they drew their identity from Him. The *shekinah* glory that represents God's presence was upon Adam and Eve in the garden; therefore, they knew no shame even though they were both naked.

Man and woman never experienced shame until after Eve ate the forbidden fruit, disobeying God's instructions. The woman was deceived, but Adam was not; he ate in rebellion.

And Adam was not deceived, but the woman being deceived, fell into transgression. (1 Timothy 2:14)

Surely something showed Adam what would happen if he ate. When Eve took the first bite, he was there and perhaps saw the glory of God depart from her. Eve did not realize that would happen. Adam, however, had watched her lose the covering and was fully aware of what would occur. Nevertheless, he opted to be with the woman rather than with God. When they ate the forbidden fruit, they felt feelings of shame for the first time. Adam and Eve had chosen to find their identity outside of God. Immediately, they saw that they were naked.

Then the eyes of both of them were opened, and they knew that they were naked; and they sewed fig leaves together and made themselves coverings. (Genesis 3:7)

Nakedness can produce feelings of shame.

"Your nakedness shall be uncovered, yes, your shame will be seen; I will take vengeance, And I will not arbitrate with a man." (Isaiah 47:3)

The first couple was embarrassed, not that some other human would view their nakedness but that God would see them lacking His glory and covering.

Centuries later, Moses also was covered with light after he saw God face-to-face.

Now it was so, when Moses came down from Mount Sinai (and the two tablets of the Testimony were in Moses' hand when he came down from the mountain), that Moses did not know that the skin of his face shone while he talked with Him. So when Aaron and all the children of Israel saw Moses, behold, the skin of his face shone, and they were afraid to come near him. . . . And when Moses had finished speaking with them, he put a veil on his face. But whenever Moses went in before the LORD to speak with Him, he would take the veil off until he came out; and he would come out and speak to the children of Israel whatever he had been commanded. And whenever the children of Israel saw the face of Moses, that the skin of Moses' face shone. Then Moses would put the veil on his face again, until he went in to speak with Him. (Exodus 34:29-35)

The exposure of nakedness to others can be evidence that the kingdom of darkness is at work. In the story of the demon-possessed man from Gadara, he wore no clothes. After his freedom he was fully clothed and in his right mind. The degree of satanic influence in a person's life often determines the degree of nakedness and shame in him or her.

Then they sailed to the country of the Gadarenes, which is opposite Galilee. And when He stepped out on the land, there met Him a certain man from the city who had demons for a long time. And he wore no clothes, nor did he live in a house but in the tombs. When he saw Jesus, he cried out, fell down before Him, and with a loud voice said, "What have I to do with You, Jesus, Son of the Most High God? I beg You, do not torment me!" For He had commanded the unclean spirit to come out of the man. . . Then they. . . found the man from whom the demons had departed, sitting at the feet of Jesus, clothed and in his right mind. And they were afraid. They also who had seen it told them by what means he who had been demon-possessed was healed. (Luke 8:26-39)

Shame can also come from feelings of loss and being exploited. People today are sometimes shamed by their appearance. Children have great pressure put on them by their peers to dress and look like everyone else. We hear statements such as these: "Why can't I have that?" "Everyone else has one!"

When I began first grade, I suffered strong feelings of shame. Because our family was so poor, I had to wear shirts my mother made for me from cattle-feed sacks. Mother did the very best she could, but I was humiliated

9

because of my appearance. As I went through elementary school, we still could not afford "stylish" clothes. I never owned a pair of Levi jeans, because they cost more than the other brands. Years later, after I had become a pastor, a lady heard this story and gave me my first pair of Levi's.

As shame came to the first couple, they became self-focused. Previously, they had been God-focused. When God asked Adam, "Where are you?", He was not seeking information. He was giving him a chance to repent of his sin. Because Adam had now become self-focused, he immediately blamed God and the woman God had given him. Adam, not only felt shame, but also felt fear for the first time. Fear and shame are very closely associated and often bound together. Most of the time, when you have shame, you will also have fear – the fear of being known.

> So he said, "I heard Your voice in the garden, and I was afraid because I was naked; and I hid myself." (Genesis 3:10)

Another result of shame is to automatically blame someone else.

> Then the man said, "The woman whom You gave to be with me, she gave me of the tree, and I ate." (Genesis 3:12)

Notice Adam blamed God rather than admitting his sin. To further justify his position, he blamed the woman also. Shame will always tempt you to blame others rather than face your own sin.[4]

Shame has a powerful influence on the whole world. Even the animal kingdom was affected by Adam's fall. The environment did not remain the same in the garden. Man and the animal kingdom experienced a separation. And Adam felt the separation from God. Just imagine the shame that came upon him every time one of his descendants would ask, "Grandpa Adam, tell us what it was like when God walked with you and Grandma Eve in the cool of the day in the garden." I am certain tears of deep regret flowed down Adam's cheeks, as he remembered how it was before shame entered his life.

Shame will always tempt you to blame others rather than face your own sin.

God is still trying to persuade us today, saying, "My sons, where are you?" But we are afraid and run away and hide. It is still the shame of failure that keeps us running from God and, as a result, not enjoying the fullness of the "cool of the day" that God has for us. So Adam was the first person, but not the last, whose identity was stolen from him.

CHAPTER TWO

EMOTIONAL INDICATORS OF SHAME

Like most works of darkness, shame operates best when it is undetected. As long as shame has freedom to move about in our lives unnoticed and unacknowledged, we can never be free. Only as we begin to identify shame at work in us are we able to understand its hold on us. As I practice the ministry of casting out demons and doing inner healing, I am absolutely convinced we must learn how to deal with shame. Otherwise, our healing and deliverance will be superficial.

Shame is like the undergarments we wear. Though they aren't on the outside for all to see, we feel a little uncomfortable if we don't have them on, because they are familiar to us. There are a number of emotional indicators of our being held captive. The shame that overtakes us then becomes automatic in our responses in life.

Below are eight indicators of emotional shame:

1 Anger
2 Sarcasm
3 Self-hatred
4 Victim mentality
5 Twisted perceptions
6 Lack of vision
7 Hopelessness
8 Cain Complex[5]

The first indicator is **anger**. I am not talking about normal anger over a specific issue. I'm talking about violent emotional outbursts, over-reactions to issues, and uncontrollable rage. I'm talking about anger when there's no known reason for it —exploding on other people with little or no provocation. It seems to be the automatic response when everything doesn't go our way. We are always "dumping" on someone.

Typically, two things happen:

1 Every time we feel anger, we feel shame-bound.

2 When shame is involved, anger is repressed. Repression is a primary, automatic ego-defense. But even then, anger clamors to be expressed. It's like keeping hungry dogs in a pen. The hungrier they get, the more we have to watch and guard the pen to keep them in. So anger is a primary indicator that a person is suffering from shame.

The second emotional indicator is the use of **sarcasm**. Sarcasm is not healthy for relationships. John Loren Sandford, founder of Elijah House Ministries, says, "Sarcasm wounds the spirit of a person and prohibits proper self-esteem." Even though it may sound funny at the moment, sarcasm is a destroyer. So if you use sarcasm in your conversations, you're motivated by shame. It will keep you striking back verbally at your family and those people you love the most. Sarcasm is never proper; it means you are tied to shame, even though you may not realize it.

> Like most works of darkness, shame operates best when it is undetected.

The third indicator is **self-hatred**, of which there are many forms. The first and foremost is self-rejection—persons who dislike some part of their body. They feel their nose is too big, their eyes are the wrong color, their hair is too curly or too straight, their ears are not shaped right. Many men and women today are not satisfied with the body God gave them. For example, look at the numbers of breast augmentation operations women are having. If you think changing the appearance of your body will cause you to accept yourself, you're deceived. Just ask the actresses in Hollywood—they go from one surgery to another trying to make themselves more attractive. Changing a body part will not cause you to accept yourself. Self-hatred is sometimes expressed by bulimia or anorexia, or even death-wishes. Many people walk a tightrope between life and death. My question is, "If you had the power to change anything about your appearance, would you use it?" If your answer is "Yes", you may be controlled by shame.

The fourth indicator that shame has captured a person is a **victim mentality**. The "poor- me" philosophy. "No one has had it as bad as me." "No one loves me." "No one wants to be my friend." "I'm a loser." "No one ever picks me for his or her team." When I first married, I was given to this. My wife, Tina, would often say to me, "Henry, why don't you stop having pity parties? No one wants to come to them, but you're inviting everyone. So why don't you quit feeling sorry for yourself?" If something goes wrong, do you wallow in your failure or your mistake? Or do you get up, dust yourself off and go on? The victim mentality never sees a way out. It's doom and gloom. Even when a helping hand is offered, the victim always has a reason why it won't work.

> Anger is a primary indicator that a person is suffering from shame.

I had a man come to me for ministry. "Jack" told me his story. His cup was never half-full; it was always half-empty. Everything I advised him to do, he had already tried or he didn't see how it would work. Thus he rejected it. All he wanted me to do was get down in the mud and wallow with him in his shame. I had been giving him biblical solutions to his problems, and he refused the word of God. So I said, "You know, I don't think God can help you." He was shocked. If you have refused God's promises for your victory, then He can't help you either. Being a victim is a terrible place to be. But you are the only one who can change your view of yourself by overcoming shame in your life.

The fifth emotional indicator is **twisted thinking**. Shame-based people often have distorted views, being almost paranoid about people not liking them. They also exaggerate rejection in their life. Shame-based people do suffer rejection but, most often, they're not being rejected as much as they think. Shame is the distorted glasses they wear. They do not see the circumstances and events from a clear, realistic perspective. Many times, this is transferred toward God. You hear statements like, "What have I done to deserve this?" Actually, they have twisted views and twisted perceptions about how life really is. Yes, everyone suffers some difficulty - the righteous as well as the wicked. But God has not singled out anyone unfairly to punish them.

The sixth emotional indicator that expresses shame is people who **lack vision.** They seem to live without direction. They cite events from the past which block their forward progress.

I ministered to Kay in an inner healing and deliverance training school. The question was asked, "What do you hope to get from this training that will help you be successful?" She said, "I couldn't be successful because I have a felony on my record, so I can't be a lawyer, I can't be a doctor and I can't be a judge." She went on and on listing the things she wouldn't be able to do. I said to her, "You told me that you dropped out of high school in the tenth grade. You can't be a lawyer, doctor or judge without high school and college degrees, and without meeting the requirements. A felony charge on your record will not keep you from being an able minister of the gospel or being able to do inner healing and deliverance. So your problem is not a felony charge."

> Until you are able to think differently, you will never act differently.

Shame causes a person to forget all of the scriptures that declare God has a future and a plan for our lives.

When there is no vision, the people perish. (Proverbs 29:18)

I have, over the years, watched numbers of people just sit and wait to die because shame robbed them of their future, their hope and their identity. However, they were not willing to take off their distorted glasses and see life from God's perspective.

The seventh indicator is a **hopelessness** that comes from the belief that "I am no longer useful to God. I have sinned so badly that He will not forgive me and no longer loves me." I was ministering to a young woman about her father-wounds, and she told me this story. Her father was an associate pastor who opened his home to a young woman he was trying to help and later had a sexual affair with her. Shame weighed so heavily on him that he left the ministry and never returned. It destroyed his life. There seemed to be no way out. He was absolutely hopeless.

The last emotional indicator is when the shame-based person takes on a **Cain complex.** "God has put a mark on me to punish me because of what I did."

And you have forgotten the exhortation which speaks to you as to sons: "My son, do not despise the chastening of the Lord,
Nor be discouraged when you are rebuked by Him;
For whom the Lord loves He chastens.
And scourges every son whom He receives"

If you endure chastening, God deals with you as with sons, for what son is there whom a father does not chasten? But if you are without chastening, of which all have become partakers, then you are illegitimate and not sons. (Hebrews 12:5-8)

God never puts a mark on believers in order to punish them. He only chastens His children because He loves us. In Scripture, punishment is reserved for the wicked. He corrects our ways so we can be successful. Shame will cause you to blame God because you don't know God for who He really is. He is a loving Father.[6]

If any of these emotional indicators control you, you can be sure that shame has captured your thinking. Until you are able to think differently, you will never act differently.

As a man thinks in his heart so is he. (Proverbs 23:7)

The hurdle to get over is to face the fact that shame is one of the major factors in your life keeping you in bondage. Because the Body of Christ has almost totally closed its eyes to the effects of shame in believers' lives, we do not hear much about it in church. When shame steals your identity, you become a different person, acting in a way that is not really you.

> When shame steals your identity, you become a different person, acting in a way that is not really you.

In dealing with shame (or true shame as we call it), we need to understand that true shame is the result of real guilt. Dealing with the guilt which comes from our sin (or missing the mark or "embarrassing events" in our life) is a process. We must experience the six R's to find complete freedom from guilt: regret, remorse, responsibility, repentance, reconciliation and relationships restored.[7] Guilt and shame will never be removed unless we have some feelings of regret, which will lead us to some degree of remorse. This causes us to accept our responsibility. In so doing, we can analyze and evaluate the scenario (and repent where necessary), which can open the door to reconciliation and broken relationships being restored. The six R's are essential to dealing with true shame in our life. Only after we deal with real guilt and true shame can we successfully tackle toxic shame. Otherwise we will not be able to discern the difference.

CHAPTER THREE

THE BONDAGE OF SHAME

A major chain which binds us is the fundamental lie, "My humanity is not good." The more one believes he or she is defective or flawed, the more one's choices in life are diminished. Remember the difference between healthy shame and toxic shame? Healthy shame says, "I have done something wrong." This acknowledgment will open the door for us to deal with the real guilt in our spirit and soul. Toxic shame, on the other hand, is the erroneous belief that I *am* wrong because I have done wrong. Toxic shame dehumanizes a person and brings spiritual bankruptcy.

When a person is truly born again by the Spirit of God, he or she experiences a new creation, and the old flawed inheritance of Adam is removed.

> Therefore, if anyone is in Christ, he is a new creation; old things have passed away; behold, all things have become new. (II Corinthians 5:17)

If this is true, God has fixed the Adamic flaw. I am again made like God – a child received into His family. Isn't that what Jesus came to do for us when He died on the cross? Why we find this hard to accept is that, once we internalize toxic shame, it becomes functionally automatic in us, triggered from within. Such shame is the unconscious demon I have never acknowledged. It will hold me in its grip until I call it by name. On the other hand, true shame is good and normal. It shows us our limits and keeps us in our boundaries. It waves a red flag and says, "You made a mistake." But shame as a healthy human emotion can be converted into toxic shame as a state of being. When that happens, your true identity is stolen from you.

Toxic shame dehumanizes a person and brings spiritual bankruptcy.

For that to happen, you must believe the lie that you are defective to the core. John Bradshaw says, "Once shame is transferred into an identity, it becomes toxic and dehumanizing."[8] Toxic shame alienates the true self from the perceived self and thus causes us to become "other-ated." The Spanish philosopher Ortegay Gasset created that term. He says, "Mankind is the only being who lives from within. Animals live in constant hyper-vigilance—always on guard, looking outside themselves for sustenance and guarding against danger. When humans no longer have an inner life, they become other-ated and dehumanized."[9]

As we stated in chapter one, shame goes back to Adam and Eve. They could get anything they needed from God. Satan's ploy was to get them to feel they had a need for something God was withholding from them. So he used comparison, saying, "You will be like God." The implication is, "You are not adequate. You need something that God will not give you." The true reality was that they were already created in the image of God. Adam and Eve fell for the lie, and then they hid from their Creator. Mankind still hides because of shame, afraid to go to God. We run from the only source of forgiveness, healing and wholeness. We have not yet learned this key to overcoming our shame, "We must name our sin in order to tame our sin."[10]

GENERATIONAL SHAME

Another way we are held in the grip of shame is through a generational curse; it is handed down to us. We just *feel* our shame. Scripture records how Lucifer led a rebellion and was cast out from heaven. (Isaiah 14:12-15) Apparently Lucifer experienced shame from his fall; for he now delights to heap it upon us. We inherit our family shame from those who went before us. Thus, man has a hole in his soul which feels like it cannot be filled up. Even when we have not violated any moral laws or ethical standards, shame seems to be ever-present. We might ask, "Has this person ever *not* known shame?" If that's the case, the person is really held captive by generational shame.

I ministered to Bill who was a good man but obsessed with making money. He loved his wife and children and said he was committed to making money *for them.* The truth is he was driven by an ancestral curse of shame. Bill was born into deep poverty. He was ashamed of his parents, their house and everything about his life. He became determined not to be poor. He was a hard worker. He chose to go to college only because he thought it would land him a better job. Now he is very successful but won't go to see his parents, because he is still ashamed of their poverty. When he was a young child, his father said, "Don't worry, son, our family has never amounted to much. So you won't have to do much to fit in." From that day forward, he was compelled to become rich. But money did not take his shame away. Bill received ministry for generational shame and broke free from a driven life. Now he can enjoy what he has made *and* his family.

The enemy uses a number of other shackles to keep us in shame. One of them is if the mother wanted to hide her pregnancy. So, as the child grows up, he does not want to be seen. We might assume he is merely timid, but he is really suffering from shame and fear, because his mother chose not to acknowledge him from the very beginning. Another avenue for shame comes from having a lot of people in the delivery room watching the birth—a "family affair". Thus, the child feels shame while still in the womb and immediately after birth. Or, if the parents and extended family are constantly talking about the pregnancy with negative or fear-filled words, shame may come to the baby.

> Mankind still hides because of shame, afraid to go to God. We run from the only source of forgiveness, healing and wholeness.

When a child is conceived with unmarried parents or is unwanted, he or she will experience shame. Deuteronomy 23:2 says that such persons will be shut out of the presence of God. This curse needs to be broken off. Although Jesus has already taken the curse of illegitimacy, we must apply that freedom by faith. If a woman conceives as a result of being raped, the child's spirit picks up the trauma, distress and shame the mother went through. If a woman attempts to abort a baby and is not successful, the child knows in its spirit. The one who was supposed to protect them has tried to kill them. This brings deep rejection. If one child in a multiple birth dies, then the others may feel shame for having lived. Oftentimes, there is one favorite picked out of multiple-birth children, thus the others feel rejected.

Another way for one to experience shame is to be born the "wrong" gender. If Daddy wanted a son and a daughter is born, especially if she is the only child, it brings great guilt and shame. She blames herself for not being the sex Daddy wanted. I've ministered to many women with deep shame because they were not born male. This is where extreme tomboys often come from. This shame is very heavy, especially in cultures where men are valued and women have no or little value.[11]

SHAME ON YOU!

Another place for shame to enter is when parents, teachers and ministers pass *their* shame to you. They may say, "Shame on you." They may compare you to your siblings, "If only you were like your brother." "If only you were beautiful like your sister." The parent tried to use shame to motivate the child. But shame comes like a hungry dog and gobbles up our identity, especially when we are teased or labeled. "You are as skinny as a beanpole." "You are fat, ugly, or dumb." Shame-based people cannot take jokes. It is amazing how many overweight people are deeply shamed by the latest "fat" joke. When people are teased, it just reinforces the lies they have already believed about themselves.

> Shame comes like a hungry dog and gobbles up our identity, especially when we are teased or labeled.

Shame can come from having unrealistic expectations placed on you. For example, when you are expected to act beyond your age, e.g., a three-year-old can never act like a five-year-old. When a child is made responsible for the care of a younger sibling and the sibling is hurt, the older child is covered with shame and receives the message, "You are not adequate."

Shame can come when the standards are raised after the task is completed. "Your report card was good, but all A's would have been much better." Shame can come when a child is punished for saying an ugly word but didn't know it was ugly. He heard Daddy say it; when he repeats it, he gets punished.

A major pathway for shame's entrance is through trauma, such as sexual or physical abuse, because abuse is extremely personal. It cuts to the bone, often leaving a person feeling completely helpless. Shame can come in dysfunctional families, through either Type-A or Type-B trauma. Type-A trauma is characterized by the lack of things that we needed – what we did not receive, e.g., hugs, kisses, and affirmation. Type-B trauma comes from hurtful, harmful things that we did receive, such as physical abuse, sexual abuse, rejection and/or abandonment.[12]

Shame has many ways to hold us but none that can't be broken. Don't let shame keep you shackled and bound. Break free, and reclaim your identity.

CHAPTER FOUR

THE SUFFERING OF SHAME

Most who suffer from the harsh hand of shame do so in silence. We're not allowed to object. It feels like a conspiracy that I get what's coming to me for what I've done and who I *feel* that I am. Many people never realize how they assist shame by not reaching out to those in pain.

In a college English class, I had to read *The Scarlet Letter* about the punishment given to a young woman caught in sexual sin. She had to wear a scarlet-colored letter "A", so everyone who saw her would know about her adultery. She suffered scorn and rejection by the townspeople. We can receive deep shame in many ways - by being a misunderstood burden-bearer, by being abandoned by family or loved ones, by rejection or neglect. No one wants to be ignored by those who are supposed to care. We all have human needs and should never be shamed for having them.

Our needs can be defined in many different terms, but most behavioral scientists agree on certain basic needs of all human beings:

1 We need unconditional love.
2 We need to feel we have intrinsic value.
3 We need to feel a measure of power in our lives.
4 We need to be acknowledged or known.
5 We need an avenue by which we can be heard so that we can feel important.

6 We need to feel we are protected by someone or more than one.

7 We need to feel we are understood when we express ourselves.[13]

If these human needs are not met, we receive shame in our spirit and soul. Our needs are God-given, not selfishness expressed. Once you are shamed, the message is that your basic needs will never be met. And if you dare to ask for them to be met, you will feel even more shamed.

> Once you are shamed, the message is that your basic needs will never be met.

Shame-based people's common trait is to go through life with wrong behavior patterns which cause them to reap more shame. It is a never-ending cycle. The alcoholic is a good example. He or she has shame from past experiences. So, he or she goes on drinking to dull the suffering of shame. Thus, he or she brings even greater shame by more wrongdoing. Another example is people in deep emotional pain. They feel shame because of it, but it drives them back to the wrong behavior which caused the pain in the first place. The cycle never ends. Shame is *not* something you should refuse to deal with.

"For whoever is ashamed of Me and My words in this adulterous and sinful generation, of him the Son of Man also will be ashamed when He comes in the glory of His Father with the holy angels." (Mark 8:38)

In essence, Jesus said, "If you won't honor Me and obey My word, I won't honor you." You have to deal with your shame. This is not optional.

There is more to getting free than casting out a demon. So what do you do with the toxic shame which comes because the kingdom of darkness wants you to suffer? You must abide in Jesus.

"Abide in Him, that when He appears, we may have confidence and not be ashamed before Him at His coming." (1 John 2:28)

SHAME AS A RESULT OF SEXUAL SIN OR ABUSE

Sexual sin or sexual abuse is one of the sources of deep shame. God created us with sexual capacity and desire. But parents, in ignorance, often link shame to sexual body parts when a child is merely curious. Little Johnny, when he is two, discovers his nose, points to it and says, "Nose!" His mother is elated and will get him to put his finger on his nose and tell everyone what it is. They all rejoice about how brilliant the child is. This is repeated with the eyes, the ears, the mouth, the toes, etc. Little Johnny is praised and applauded for being a genius. One day, with a houseful of company for the Christmas party, Johnny is getting a late bath and discovers his penis. Because of all the past praise, he is sure that Mom will be just as excited about his knowing the name of this body part. He runs naked into the living room, holding his penis in his hand, and shouts, "Look, my pee-pee!" Mother screams, grabs him by the ear and moves quicker than Johnny has ever seen, saying, "Shame on you! Don't ever do that again." Punishment comes swift and sure, and Johnny now internalizes. Thus, he must disown his body parts. What he thought his parents would be happy about now becomes a source of shame.

> Most who suffer from the harsh hand of shame do so in silence.

Often children who are sexually abused by parents or grandparents are told they can never talk about it. "This is our secret." And if children are told, "I'm doing this to you because I love you," love becomes twisted and shameful for them. They are forced to suffer in silence.

How does a girl rid herself of sexual shame? In 2 Samuel 13, the story is told of King David's children, Amnon and Tamar, his half-sister. Amnon, consumed with lust for Tamar, tricked her by faking being sick and then asking her to cook for him. When she did, he attempted to rape her. Tamar said, in verses 12-13, *"Do not do this disgraceful thing. Where could I take my shame?"* Amnon refused to listen to her and went ahead and violated her. She ran crying and distraught from her brother's home and suffered in silence.

Such violations by those who are a part of our support system bring deep shame on us. We feel we are worthless. Toxic shame sets in, stealing our identity. Sexual sins of incest, rape and abuse stay with a person the rest of their life. Where do you take your shame? You suffer in silence and anonymity.[14] Statistics tell us that one out of every four women will be sexually abused before the age of 16. We're letting the kingdom of darkness take away the value and self-esteem of our women. Shame is a master emotion because it can internalize all other emotions – such as fear and rejection. Shame must be seen as a great enemy to the plans of God.

Parents must be extremely careful not to transfer their own shame to their children when their children make a mistake. How do parents shame a child? By saying:

1 "What you did is very, very bad!"
2 "Don't ever let me catch you touching yourself like that again."
3 "Go put on some decent clothes."
4 "Cover your private parts – that is ugly and nasty; don't ever do that again."

These types of statements are meant to motivate the child by shame. Parents say such things because of their own shame. The parent has suffered all these years under the load of shame, and it is an automatic response to put shame on others.[15]

Shame is carefully hidden beneath the surface of many successful people. They are praised and admired for their talents, their gifts, and their super-achievements. They seem strong and self-assured, but behind their masks lurk depression, shame and a host of other negative feelings. Even many rich, beautiful and famous Hollywood stars are driven by shame. Shame has even driven people to commit suicide. Many eating disorders and other fleshly appetites which cannot be satisfied have their roots in shame. It is the unseen force which causes people to bow their head and suffer in silence, while desperately trying to keep their "mask" in place.

THE VARIABLES OF SHAME

CHAPTER FIVE

STOLEN IDENTITY

Christians recognize the characteristics of their true self in the story of the life of Jesus. He is what we could be if we followed fully the plan God has for us. We also see some of our true self in the lives of our heroes and our saints. When we can feel the pressure of our conscience working right, the emotion of good shame guides us to be a better person. A healthy sense of shame is perhaps the best sign of our divine origin. We desire to rise to the level of our intended creation. The person we are today never quite matches the person we know we are designed to be.

Lewis Smedes maintains that there are five ingredients of our true self:

1. We are grateful
2. We are an integrated whole.
3. We are discerning.
4. We are in charge of our life.
5. We are a true lover.[16]

Shame comes into our life when we are aware that our actual self is not the same as our true self. As we *focus* in on this difference in our life, false (or toxic) shame will take root. Toxic shame saps our joy and steals our creativity. Thus I am forced to wear a mask rather than be the real person I am. The reason we choose to wear a mask is two-fold:

1 We are hiding from other people.

2 We are hiding from God.

We may deceive other people with our mask; they may look at us and accept us. But we can't hide from God. He's really on both sides of our mask. Satan wants to make our feelings of inadequacy so strong we can never

Toxic shame saps our joy and steals our creativity.

get free. Toxic shame can lead to all sorts of neuroses and character disorders. The neurotic person assumes too much responsibility. The person with a character disorder does not assume enough responsibility. When neurotic people are in conflict with other people, the neurotic person automatically assumes that he or she is at fault. When the person with character disorders is in conflict with other people, he or she automatically assumes that other people are at fault.[17]

Development of Toxic Shame

All of us have some smatterings of character disorder and neurotic behavior, but the major problem in our life is to detect and classify our personal responsibility. We must be committed to a life of honesty, love and discipline and thus live in reality. A toxic-shame-based person has an adversarial relationship first with himself and then with others. He must wear a mask. When wearing the mask – being a false self, one ceases to be an authentic person or human being. He becomes a human doing.[18] A toxic-shame-based person will avoid exposing himself to others or to himself. Such a person will admit guilt, hurt, fear or pain before admitting shame. Toxic shame produces feelings of isolation. The person is haunted by a sense of absence and emptiness. We struggle with the fear of failure, but we do not realize it is shame which causes us to fail. I can take the loss, but I can't take the shame that comes from the loss.

The problem with wearing a mask too long is I forget who I really am—my true self. I begin to believe I am the mask I wear. My identity is stolen. So what do shame-based people really look like? They look like you and me. Toxic shame lies at the core of many emotional disorders that produce disturbing inner states. It is the closest thing to defining human bondage I know.[19] So we can use shame as a catch-all to encompass many of our emotional difficulties.

Adam symbolizes the human race. The Bible suggests that Adam was not satisfied with himself. He wanted to be more than a human. That's how Satan got Adam to look at the creation rather than to God. Scripture suggests that the original human bondage - our original sin - is the desire to be someone other than who we really are. That's toxic shame. Once Adam chose that, he became naked and ashamed. The unconditional love and acceptance of our true self seems to be the hardest of all tasks for human beings. So we try to create a more powerful *false* self or just give up and become less than human. It takes tons of energy and hard work to live up to a false self-life.

> The problem with wearing a mask too long is I forget who I really am.

Toxic shame will not let you invest yourself in meaningful relationships. You internalize your shame; you *become* shame. We all know people who are angry or sad or fearful people. Their particular emotion has become a part of their false character. They no longer have sadness or anger; they are melancholy, they are angry. John Bradshaw says there are at least three steps to the process of internalizing shame:

Step 1 Identification with unreliable and shame-based models.

Step 2 The trauma of abandonment and the binding of feelings, needs and drives with shame.

Step 3 The interconnection of memory imprints which forms collages of shame.[20]

If your parents were shame-based, you took on the family's shame as you reached out to identify with them. One way shame comes is through improper parenting. Parents often scold a child far more than he deserves. Harsh punishment and improper judgment can come from a wounded parent or one trained in legalism. Parents shame their children. Friends shame other friends. Teachers seeking to motivate students shame them.

Most of the peer pressure children receive today is really shame-based. We allow family rackets as a cover for shame. A racket is a family-authorized feeling used to replace a non-acceptable and shameful feeling.[21] A common example of a female racket is crying. We allow women to cry, which is acceptable, rather than to express their anger. Parents will often convert their anger into making their children feel guilty when they do not do what the parents want. Then, the parents will react with anger to their children's expressions of fear, sadness or anger.

> If your parents were shame-based, you took on the family's shame as you reached out to identify with them.

It may be that much criminal behavior is due to toxic shame which leads to repetition—the compulsion to do what was done to us. Toxic shame is the fuel for the massive problem of addiction that we have today.[22]

We have sixty million sexually abused victims. We have seventy-five million seriously affected by alcoholism. We have fifteen million families who suffer from violent activities. We have thirteen million who are addicted gamblers. Sixty percent of women suffer from eating disorders. As mentioned earlier, one out of four women will suffer sexual abuse by the age of sixteen. Sexual abuse of boys is quickly becoming just as common and is equally destructive. Because we live in a society which has lost its identity, we suffer from shame. Therefore we are no longer human beings, but rather human doings, wearing masks and pretending to be people we are really not.

CHAPTER SIX

PUSHING SHAME BUTTONS

Why is it so important for us to shame others? It goes back to the principle, "hurt people hurt other people." I learned this when I was about nine or ten years old. I had a half-collie and half-Australian sheepdog named Dusty that I truly loved. On the farm in North Louisiana where I was raised, we had cows, horses, pigs and chickens. Dusty knew the name of every cow in the field. If she was so instructed, Dusty could bring one particular cow, or the whole herd, home to the barn. I was always attentive to her and took care of her. One evening, she did not show up for her food. I was quite concerned. And the next morning, she was not there. When I went to look for her, I found her in the back field with her back leg caught in the fence. She had been there all night. She had tried to jump the fence and got caught. I rushed up to free her, but she bit me. I was totally startled! She was my best friend. I truly loved her. Why did she bite me? I rushed back home and told my mother what had happened. Being the wise woman she was, Mother said, "She bit you out of fear. Now go get the wire cutters. Get on the opposite side of the fence and cut her free, and she will be all right." I did as my mother instructed me. I climbed over the fence and cut her free. When this was completed, she came and licked me in the face, showing her love and appreciation.

People are like hurt animals. They will strike out at you in their pain, because of their heavy load of shame. Shame damages our hearts. Teenagers insult each other because of it. Phrases like, "You are such a loser" are often used. This statement is not about one's behavior; it is about one's worth.[23] Vulnerable teens are trying to find their real self and become who they really are. Statements like this trigger shame. Teenagers have become masters of punching the "shame buttons" of other teens. Don't let other shame-based people push *your* buttons.

> When we hear a lie long enough, we will begin to believe that it is the truth.

How many people feel that they are losers? Probably more than we realize, teens *and* adults are gripped by such feelings. Somewhere along the way, most people feel like a loser. Sometimes it takes only that big shove in the wrong direction to push us over the edge. My shame should never be a cause for me to bring you down.

> Indeed let no one who waits in faith on you be ashamed. Let those be ashamed who deal treacherously without cause. (Psalm 25:3)

Satan will never miss an opportunity to shame you. When we hear a lie long enough, we will begin to believe that it is the truth. Then toxic shame sets into our lives.

In 1 Samuel 20, we read about King Saul bringing shame on his son Jonathan because he was seeking to protect David. King Saul disgraced Jonathan in front of the royal court by calling him the son of a perverse, rebellious woman. Thus Jonathan's anger was triggered because of that embarrassment. Then Jonathan's *shame* was also triggered when shame was brought to his close friend David.

> Then David hid in the field. And when the New Moon had come, the king sat down to eat the feast. Now the king sat on his seat, as at other times, on a seat by the wall. And Jonathan arose, and Abner sat by Saul's side, but David's place was empty. Nevertheless Saul did not say anything that day, for he thought, "Something has happened to him; he is unclean, surely he is unclean." And it happened the next day, the second day of the month, that David's place was empty. And Saul said to Jonathan his son, "Why has the son of Jesse not come to eat, either yesterday or today?"

So Jonathan answered Saul, "David earnestly asked permission of me to go to Bethlehem. And he said, 'Please let me go, for our family has a sacrifice in the city, and my brother has commanded me to be there. And now, if I have found favor in your eyes, please let me get away and see my brothers' Therefore he has not come to the king's table."

Then Saul's anger was aroused against Jonathan, and he said to him, "You son of a perverse, rebellious woman! Do I not know that you have chosen the son of Jesse to your own shame and to the shame of your mother's nakedness? For as long as the son of Jesse lives on the earth, you shall not be established, nor your kingdom. Now therefore, send and bring him to me, for he shall surely die." And Jonathan answered Saul his father, and said to him, "Why should he be killed? What has he done?" Then Saul cast a spear at him to kill him, by which Jonathan knew that it was determined by his father to kill David. So Jonathan arose from the table in fierce anger, and ate no food the second day of the month, for he was grieved for David, because his father had treated him shamefully. (1 Samuel 20:24-34)

King Saul was enraged because of his own shame, which caused him to deeply shame his son, and that created a division between them. Shame will separate you from your family and loved ones.[24]

SHAME IN THE NEW TESTAMENT

Jesus' love for others stirred up the shame of the synagogue rulers. They covered their shame by performance and legalism. Jesus exposed their shame and they reacted in anger.

Now He was teaching in one of the synagogues on the Sabbath. And behold, there was a woman who had a spirit of infirmity eighteen years, and was bent over and could in no way raise herself up. But when Jesus saw her, He called her to Him and said to her, "Woman, you are loosed from your infirmity." And He laid His hands on her, and immediately she was made straight, and glorified God. But the ruler of the synagogue answered with indignation, because Jesus had healed on the Sabbath; and he said to the crowd, "There are six days on which men ought to work; therefore come and be healed on them, and not on the Sabbath day." The Lord then answered him and said, "Hypocrite! Does not each one of you on the Sabbath loose his ox or donkey from the stall, and lead it away to water it? So ought not this woman, being a daughter of Abraham, whom Satan has bound — think of it — for eighteen years, be loosed from this bond on the Sabbath?" And when He said these things, all His adversaries were put to shame; and all the multitude rejoiced for all the glorious things that were done by Him. (Luke 13:10-17)

Jesus' act of love angered the Pharisees, and they rebuked Him for it. The Pharisees were shamed for their lack of love, and their response was anger and rejection.

Paul instructed believers to live in such a manner that no one could bring shame on them.

Likewise, exhort the young men to be sober-minded, in all things showing yourself to be a pattern of good works; in doctrine showing integrity, reverence, incorruptibility, sound speech that cannot be condemned, that one who is an opponent may be ashamed, having nothing evil to say of you. (Titus 2:6-8)

So we are to live in such a way that those who oppose the gospel of Christ have no occasion to punch our "shame buttons". This can be done only if we walk in love and are free from toxic shame.

Our enemies cannot bring shame on us if we have dealt with it in our own lives. We need to be prepared to answer our critics for the way we live and function.

But sanctify the Lord God in your hearts, and always be ready to give a defense to everyone who asks you a reason for the hope that is in you, with meekness and fear; having a good conscience, that when they defame you as evildoers, those who revile your good conduct in Christ may be ashamed. (1 Peter 3:15-16)

Many times, Christians try to shame other believers for the way they practice the scriptures. It is amazing to me how deeply shame controls people's actions and binds them to their traditions. Many who believe in and practice spiritual gifts today are shunned and some are even disfellowshipped. This is a shame-button for some religious fundamentalists and ultra-conservatives. I've seen life-long friendships destroyed, families separated, division lines drawn because someone embraced the practice of spiritual gifts. We try to cover our shame by proving that others are wrong.

> We try to cover **our** shame by proving that others are wrong.

We are invited to bring true shame on those who depart from the faith, so that they'll return. We are never to be that person's enemy but always remain a brother. What was so important that we are instructed to shame a fellow believer? False doctrine. Many believers bring shame on themselves because they have believed wrong doctrine.

> But as for you, brethren, do not grow weary in doing good. And if anyone does not obey our word in this epistle, note that person and do not keep company with him, that he may be ashamed. (2 Thessalonians 3:13-14)

We bring shame on ourselves and on the name of God when we sue a fellow believer in a court of law. Our own shame stops us from suffering for Jesus' sake.

> Dare any of you, having a matter against another, go to law before the unrighteous, and not before the saints? Do you not know that the saints will judge the world? And if the world will be judged by you, are you unworthy to judge the smallest matters? Do you not know that we shall judge angels? How much more, things that pertain to this life? If then you have judgments concerning things pertaining to this life, do you appoint those who are least esteemed by the church to judge? I say this to your shame. Is it so, that there is not a wise man among you, not even one, who will be able to judge between his brethren? But brother goes to law against brother, and that before unbelievers! Now therefore, it is already an utter failure for you that you

go to law against one another. Why do you not rather accept wrong? Why do you not rather let yourselves be cheated? No, you yourselves do wrong and cheat, and you do these things to your brethren! Do you not know that the unrighteous will not inherit the kingdom of God? Do not be deceived. Neither fornicators, nor idolaters, nor adulterers, nor homosexuals, nor sodomites, nor thieves, nor covetous, nor drunkards, nor revilers, nor extortioners will inherit the kingdom of God. (1 Corinthians 6:1-10)

Shame brings addictions. The driving force in many addictions is our broken self. We have received toxic shame, and our belief system is flawed. We believe the lie that we are an intrinsically flawed person. So the real me is broken or refused, and I create a false me in its place to try to gain acceptance.[25] Look at the example of the workaholic, trying to be intimate with work, because he or she cannot be intimate with God or another person. The alcoholic drinks because he has tried and failed to be intimate with others. We all have a great need to be intimate with God and with another person. If I cannot be intimate with a real woman, I will turn to pornography or some other form of sexual addiction—a false intimacy. This brings additional shame to me and to others. An addiction is an attempt to avoid loneliness and hurt, which is the under-belly of shame and that comes because I don't love myself. Why? Because I do not see myself as God sees me. My identity has been stolen.

> We believe the lie that we are an intrinsically flawed person.

CHAPTER SEVEN

HIDDEN FENCES OF SHAME

God created mankind with free will so he could choose to follow his heart in voluntary obedience. God designed the man and woman to live together in love and unity. He also planned that children, extended families and friends live together in open fellowship and community. Ever since creation, the devil has attempted to erect fences and barriers to separate us from God and from one another. One of the great barriers between us and God is shame. Shame not only fences me out from God, but it also fences other people out from me. People know only my mask; they do not know the real me.

What are some of the fences that shame seeks to place in our lives? One is poverty. Even if we are born into a Christian home, our environment seeks to dictate our value to us. If my family is poor, I will find it difficult not to accept the world's perspective of who I am. My poverty says I am worth little; therefore, I feel shame. If I cannot dress like others, do things they do and go places they go, I may feel I have less value. My ability to achieve in life will usually depend on my opportunity for education. Many young men and women never make it out of the "poor" neighborhood, because they see no way to do it. The cycle keeps repeating itself. People in poverty may act like crabs in a bucket. When one is nearing the top to escape, the others will reach up and pull him back into the bucket. The environment has successfully kept you in place to repeat the cycle again and again. Likewise, Christians sometimes do not need the world to wound them; other Christians will do it. If we don't have someone from outside the church wounding us, we ourselves will wound one another.[26]

Sadly, parents can be the ones who build shame fences in a child's life. Parents are either your greatest asset or your greatest enemy. This depends on how much shame they themselves have received and kept. If they cannot eliminate toxic shame in their own lives, it will severely limit their parenting abilities. Parents who are shame-based can never let you grow up and be free from shame.[27] They can never see your need to get what is essential to thrive. It is like the coal miner who says, "My son will take my place in the mine when I am gone." Parents often walk through life with blinders on and can't see that their child needs to walk a different path. Parents may desire good for their children, but they can be the fence that keeps them locked up in the old way of life.

Teachers can provide another barrier to keep us from freeing ourselves. Teachers are often so shame-based that they use words of condemnation and ridicule to keep students in line. Teachers do need to exercise control in the class for order and direction, but they also may use it to cover their own insecurities and fears. The more gifted a student is, the more condemnation and shame it takes to keep them from "making waves." Teachers wound the child with words like, "You can do better," "You're not working up to your potential," "You are lazy, stupid"—negative words that bring shame. Praise and encouragement provide greater motivation for improvement. Remember, God calls us saints even when our temporary behavior may not affirm it!

> Shame not only fences me out from God, but it also fences other people out from me.

Another fence to scale is one built by your friends and peers. A person who dares you to do something wrong or harmful is not your friend. Many a young boy has been shamed through sexual activities at a sleep-over because someone called him "chicken" if he would not participate. Once a child gets so labeled, it seems the devil always keeps bringing up other scenarios so people will call him "chicken". He is shamed to the core and sees himself as such.

As I was growing up in school, there was a young man named Sam. He was not the athletic type but leaned more toward art and music. He was preyed on by some of the older boys who forced him to commit sodomy. He then was called names and teased and was greatly shamed. This reputation followed him. He was taken advantage of time and time again. He could not wait to leave home and escape his shame. Unfortunately, his shame went with him for it was now inside him.

> God calls us saints
> even when our
> temporary behavior
> may not affirm it!

Another fence to climb is illegitimate birth. This fence of shame is built on the inside. These feelings come from the child's spirit, not necessarily his mind or from others' mouths.

> One of illegitimate birth shall not enter the assembly of the LORD; even to the tenth generation none of his descendants shall enter the assembly of the LORD. (Deuteronomy 23:2)

Even if a person is not aware of the illegitimacy, he is affected - often fearful, full of rejection and feelings of abandonment, but not knowing why. Such persons may find it difficult to get into God's presence in worship. They know God is there, but somehow it seems they can't get in touch with Him. They feel less valued than others.

A couple brought their eight year old son to me. Jim was afraid of the dark and in general was fearful about life. As I ministered to the father and mother (which is my custom before I minister to a child), I asked about his conception. They both said the wife was pregnant before they married. As I ministered to Jim, I broke the curse of illegitimacy and then pulled down the stronghold of fear. Jim is now in his late teens and shows no signs of drawing back from life. The fence of illegitimacy can be torn down.

Another fence is divorce—a cruel taskmaster, bringing shame on the innocent. Children suffer greatly when a marriage is broken apart, often feeling they are the cause. Imagine the burden that comes when a child is shuttled back and forth between the parents, weekend after weekend. For some shame hovers over them like a cloud because they never see their father. When other children ask questions such as, "Why doesn't your dad ever attend your ballgames?" the child feels ashamed and different. Even today, when divorce is becoming the rule rather than the exception, shame is like a slap in the face.

In the first grade, I was extremely ashamed. I was the only child in my class from a "broken home" as it was then called. Divorce wasn't acceptable in 1947. I was a "marked" child, and some children were not allowed to play with me or to be my friend. They said I had bad blood. I remember asking my mother, "What is bad blood?" How do you explain this to a seven year old child? My mother tried to ease my pain the best she could, but the answer was not sufficient.

These are just a few fences which have to be dealt with, as shame claims its victims. The dynamic core of our human life is in our feelings, our needs and our drives. When these are bound by shame, then we are disgraced to our very core, alienated from ourselves as well as from others. Shame will cause a person to compartmentalize his life. Suppose you were raised under the false doctrine that Christians are never to be angry. If you begin to express anger in your childhood and your parents attack you for it, you immediately alienate the shame of anger from who you are. You disown this part of yourself, because there is no way to safely express anger. You do this to please your parents. You have formed a compartment in your life to contain your anger. When shame has thus become fully internalized, nothing about yourself is okay. You feel flawed and inferior. You now have a sense of being a failure. Now you take steps toward non-reality.[29]

> Statements which attack the person's being bring great shame and build dividing walls.

In marriage, we develop techniques to shame our spouses. Statements like this put up a fence. "Being married to you is like being married to a seventh grader." "In our marriage, I have three children—my two daughters and my husband." Statements which attack the person's being bring great shame and build dividing walls. These techniques come from a desire to control. Two major demons which play into shame are 1) confusion and 2) misdirection. Satan capitalizes on confusion in our lives—we don't know which way to go or what to do. So we do nothing, or we do the wrong thing. Either one spells defeat.

How do we maintain these strongholds of shame?

1 We are continually faced with false standards. Our society gives us a lot of wrong information on how to solve our problems. You don't ask a man who's been divorced four times how to handle your marital problems with your wife. You'll get wrong standards, wrong instruction and wrong information. Most of us are on the merry-go round of shame, and we don't know how to get off.

2 Our media constantly floods us with lies that we will be better off if we *buy* something. It is "what we don't have" that under girds our shame. Advertisement enforces our mask. I will go into this in more detail in Division 3.

3 Society uses comparison to others and their accomplishments to prove *we* are not worthy. We don't "measure up" if we can't do certain things. This is the same lie Lucifer told Eve in the garden, "You are missing out by not knowing good *and* evil." Eve fell for the lie, and here we are today - still gripped by shame and nakedness.[30]

We desire to move forward but are kept in place by our fences. We develop a mask to make us feel comfortable, but we still live in misery.

CHARACTERISTICS OF SHAME

How do you know if you are suffering from shame? After you read this chapter, you can look at your life and you will know if you are under the bondage of shame. Of course, you may not necessarily have all of these characteristics.

CHARACTERISTIC 1 – COMPULSION

If you are a shame-based person, you may have a compulsion to help others. You become a "good Samaritan". This driving force to help others is to keep you from feeling the pain of your own shame. To have value, I must help those in need. If I don't, I have no worth and will feel the pain of my own shame. Therefore, I am driven to help others in need.

CHARACTERISTIC 2 – ANGER

When you see a person being bullied, you feel anger stirring deep within you. What pulls this trigger? If you don't rescue this underdog, your shame-pain will rise up. You recall the times you were unjustly treated. If, in some way, you can help those who are being taken advantage of, you can keep your shame in its cage. In the first grade, my best friend was bullied by twin boys from the second grade. They charged him 25 cents to polish his new shoes, but they used mud and water instead of shoe polish. He came to me, crying about what had happened. I went to them and demanded his money back. The twins wanted to fight. So we fought, and I won. I recovered, not only *his* money, but that which they had taken from all the other kids they had deceived.

CHARACTERISTIC 3 – PERFORMANCE

Performance-oriented people *work* in order to be loved. God - and everyone else - loves me only if I perform. I have believed this lie because that's how I felt loved by my parents. I was rewarded when I succeeded. If I feel I have to *earn* love from people, I believe God demands the same thing. However, God loves us—not for what we do, but for who we are, His children. Actually, He loved us even when we were His enemies.

CHARACTERISTIC 4 – CONTROL

Shame-based people feel the need to be in control at all times, so nothing will happen that embarrasses or shames them. When the five-year-old child of such a parent acts out in public, they immediately shame the child. If the child says a curse word in a crowded place, the response will be, "We don't talk that way; I'd better never hear you say that again." The child was merely repeating a word he had heard his parents say. The parent will shame rather than instruct.

CHARACTERISTIC 5 – LOST IDENTITY

Many deeply shamed people so lose their own identity that they must live through other people. I find many sexually abused women in this state. They are known for what their father did or what their husband does. They have no real identity or purpose of their own. "I am the president's wife," as if she didn't have a name, or "I am Mrs. John Smith." People create love addictions and become the appendage of another person. They are ashamed of who they are or, perhaps, feel they are not allowed to be who they are. Therefore, they unwittingly take the other person's identity for their own.[31]

CHARACTERISTIC 6 – SHAMING TECHNIQUES

Shame-based people develop techniques to shame other people. You become the judge of right and wrong in the lives of others. When someone triggers your shame, you must confront—at any cost. You just can't let that person get by with what he or she said or did. You have elected yourself to set the record straight. Your shame will not let you be silent.

CHARACTERISTIC 7 – FILTERS

You filter all incoming information and compare yourself with others. You are always listening, filtering, storing data, so you can rank yourself in society, church, school or family. You can never relax and just enjoy being with anyone. You must be on guard to cover your shame.

CHARACTERISTIC 8 – STANDARDS

The shame-based person is always examining present standards of acceptance and trying to push them up. The advertising media always help you in this project. There are always new criteria to evaluate. "Where did you buy those shoes, Neiman Marcus or Lord and Taylor?" If they weren't bought there, that's not good enough. Shame drives us to keep reaching for higher and higher standards.

CHARACTERISTIC 9 – NEGATIVE FOCUSES

Our "shame radar" scans only the negative. The other person can have ten good character traits and two not so good, but we will see only the two negatives. Only occasionally may a positive trait be mentioned. Shame must expose the negative. In so doing, shame is strengthened.

CHARACTERISTIC 10 – NO BELONGING

Shame-based people always feel they are on the outside looking in. Even if they have been asked to belong, shame blocks the doorway and keeps them out. They won't accept your invitation because they feel worthless, and worthless people can't ever belong.

CHARACTERISTIC 11 – SUICIDE

People who lose hope and take their own lives have been overtaken by shame. Suicide is the ultimate rejection of self, of others and of God. Only shame and hopelessness can take people to this place in their life.[32]

CHARACTERISTIC 12 – EATING DISORDERS

A person who is anorexic or bulimic has believed a lie. They are ashamed of what they *think* they look like. We all know that a truly anorexic person is just skin and bones, yet they see themselves as fat and ugly. Perhaps somewhere along the way, an authority figure has labeled the person fat and ugly, and it brought shame, which then worked on the mind until the person's self-perception became distorted. Not all eating disorders are shame-based, but many are. Other factors - fear, control, perfectionism - contribute to bringing about the eating disorder.

CHARACTERISTIC 13 – ANOTHER IDENTITY

The young person who is forced to perform a certain way for father's approval and a different way for mother's and yet even another way for acceptance by friends is in great confusion. This causes one to create separate identities for various people, and it brings great turmoil in his or her spirit. The following verse links shame and confusion.

> Let those be put to shame and brought to dishonor who seek after my life; Let those be turned back and brought to confusion who plot my hurt. (Psalm 35:4 – Verse 26 restates this thought in a slightly different way.)

I can't always perform in the expected manner and, when I fall short, I heighten my shame.

CHARACTERISTIC 14 – LACK OF BOUNDARIES

A person driven by shame has no boundary system. There are universal boundaries we all observe. For example, we have men's and women's restrooms, and we observe those boundaries. If you cross that boundary, you will feel shame. I well remember a moment of embarrassment for me. My wife and I were returning home from a trip to visit family. We were traveling unusually late, and I badly needed to use the restroom. I pulled into the first gas station we found, jumped out and dashed into the restroom. I was in the stall when I heard my wife come in. I said, "What are you doing in the men's room?" She answered, "This is the women's restroom. Why are you in here?"

I said to her, "Hold the door, and do not let anyone in until I am done." I had broken a universal boundary which all people respect, and I felt shame. If we do not have boundaries, we will allow others to transgress our space. This happens when fathers do not respect their daughters in the bathroom, or mothers their sons, or when siblings don't honor each other. Boundaries are crossed when we do not separate our children, at the appropriate age for bathing. And there comes a time when Dad should no longer give his daughter a bath. Shame arises when boundaries are violated.

Here's a young man who has been off to college and is on his way home for Thanksgiving dinner. His mother has told him to be there at noon sharp, but he has a history of being late. Sure enough, the appointed time comes, and he is not there. One o'clock comes... The reason? He had a car accident on the way home—just a fender bender, but it delayed him for about an hour and a half. As he rushes in the door, he is wondering, "What is my mother going to say?" She doesn't ask why he is late; she just unloads her anger on him. Because of past shame and the lack of a proper boundary system, he takes what mother dishes out. He tells her about the accident later, after she has shamed him completely for not being on time.

CHARACTERISTIC 15 – HOPELESSNESS

When we lose hope, that is evidence that we have embraced shame.

> Such hope never disappoints or deludes or shames us, for God's love has been poured out in our hearts through the Holy Spirit who has been given to us. (Romans 5:5 AMP.)

We can't walk in God's love and be without hope. If you have no hope, then shame has consumed your life. The feeling of hopelessness is not for the true believer, because Jesus has given us an eternal hope. I may lose my hope for a moment, but I can't lose all my hope. My hope is in Jesus and what He has done for me.[33]

CHARACTERISTIC 16 – CONFUSION

If your life is filled with confusion, you are likely shame-based. Confusion keeps us from making clear decisions and from properly relating to other people. Our wandering around without purpose and/or direction can be the result of being controlled by shame.

Characteristic 17 – Self-Pity

Do you feel you've had it worse than most people? Nobody really likes you or loves you? Nobody will pick you for their team? Do you turn inward and blame what is happening to you now on what occurred in the past? If so, self-pity rules your life because of toxic shame. Self-pity is not a pretty garment. It never looks good on people. Self-pity makes you turn inward, shut other people out and not see God's best for your life. It causes you to wallow in the defeats and hurts of your past.

Characteristic 18 – Hypersensitivity to Criticism

Shame-based people are given over to criticism of others, but you dare not be critical of them. They cannot handle it. For them, there is no such thing as corrective or constructive criticism. In essence, their mindset is, "If you criticize me, you don't like me. You are cutting me down. You are trying to destroy me." Every word is taken personally. Criticism can never provide an answer to their inadequacies.

Characteristic 19 – Self-focused

Shame-based people feel everyone else sees all of their imperfections and their faults. They may notice two friends talking to each other, and shame says, "They are talking about *me*!" This is really inverted arrogance. Such people often fear being in social settings because they just *know* everyone is looking at them and talking about them. But you can see how this keeps them from meaningful relationships.

Characteristic 20 – Appearance

Shame-based people put a high value on their appearance. If they don't look like they just stepped out of Vogue or GQ magazine, they do not want to be seen. Every hair must be in place, every bit of clothing properly adjusted. They base their value on what they look like, not on what God says about them. You know the old saying: "Clothes make the man!" That is a lie right out of hell. You can put a $2,000 suit on a murderer, but that does not make him a good person! It takes character, not clothes, to make a man. Shame-based people must have a pat on the back. How long does that last? Only as long as the hand is on the back—no longer. Yet they strive and connive for approval, and appearance is a big part of that.

CHARACTERISTIC 21 – UNFULFILLED

Being unfulfilled is a driving force in the life of a shame-based person—never satisfied with what they have or what they do. Instead, they gripe and complain about what they did not get done. Nothing is ever enough. When John D. Rockefeller was the richest man in America, he was asked, "Sir, which million brought the most satisfaction to you?" His answer was, "The next one." Shame drives the rich and the poor. The lack of being satisfied leads to addictions—workaholism, alcoholism, the need for fame and fortune.

CHARACTERISTIC 22 – FEAR OF RELATIONSHIPS

Shame keeps walls up in our life. We are afraid to let anyone in, because they might see who we really are—without our mask. "I must keep my spouse at arm's length." "I must not be found out." "I must build my walls stronger and taller." It is like a man newly married, who wore a hairpiece. He never took it off except at night after the lights were out. He would lay it very neatly on the nightstand and put it on again before sunrise. He was afraid his wife would find out he was bald. How long can he keep up that charade? Sooner or later, he *will* be exposed. Shame-based people cannot face their fears—or reality.

CHARACTERISTIC 23 – EMOTIONLESS

Certain shame-based people shut off their emotions because feelings are often painful, so they "stuff them". This is more common with men than with women because, due to our macho male culture, men consider emotions a sign of weakness. Little boys are told, "Men don't cry." "That didn't hurt." "Suck it up." "Act like a man." "Don't be a sissy."

A brother came to me for ministry. Carl told me how he and his wife had heated discussions about being "emotional in religion" as he put it. "I just don't have emotions," he said. "But my wife tries to get me to be emotional.

She cries about things and she wants me to cry about things." He could not talk about emotions with another woman, even his wife, so he opted to close off that part of himself. As we started our ministry time, I led him through inner healing for the wounds he received as a child from his mother. As I did, he burst into tears and sobbed. He had stuffed his emotions down and for years acted as if they weren't there. Feeling his emotions had been far too painful to him, but now he is set free.

CHARACTERISTIC 24 – ARROGANCE

Many shame-based people hide behind pride and arrogance in their lives. They put others down; they must feel superior. A man might stay lost for hours on end, even with his family begging for him to ask for directions. He will say, "I'm not lost! I'm just taking the long way around; I know where I am. Leave me alone. I'll get there." It is never wrong to admit we don't know where we are going. But, if I am shame-based, I will not be able to put down my pride and ask someone else to help me. I cannot admit that I need help because I must keep up the appearance that I am independent and do not need anyone – even to give me directions.[34]

All these characteristics can help us identify shame in our life. Obviously, we don't have to have all of them to have a shame-based life. If you have only one, why not work on that one and get free from it. Keeping your mask in place is a full-time job, but it will always end in failure.

Where did we learn all of this shame-based activity? From our family of origin. Parents teach it to their children, because it was taught to them. We will never break the cycle of shame unless God intervenes and shows us a better way of life.[35]

CHAPTER NINE

MAINTAINING SHAME

The kingdom of darkness has set in place rules that keep shame coming, generation after generation. Toxic shame is fostered primarily in significant relationships. Only someone you value can bring shame to you. Suppose you're in your car going down the highway and another driver you do not know expresses anger at how you're driving. They curse you, call you dirty names, and even make angry gestures. But that does not really hurt or shame you. However, if your spouse, whom you love, did that, you would be deeply shamed because of your relationship. In essence, your spouse would be ascribing a lack of value to you. If your self-value is low and your spouse's words reflect an even lower value, this confirms the shame you already have.

Toxic shame is multi-generational in its scope. When two people who are already shame-based get married, their relationship will be governed by the core of shame. They have already erected walls to protect and separate. A major factor in such a marriage is a lack of intimacy. They will live together but never *be* together. You can never let someone get close to you if you feel you are flawed to the core. The only spouse they will ever know is the mask each one wears. Shame-based marriages maintain non-intimacy through poor communications, non-productive fighting, games, manipulation, control, withdrawal, blaming and confluence.[36] Confluence is the agreement never to disagree. Confluence produces pseudo-intimacy but never a real intimacy. It is amazing how many people are willing to live in shallow water and call it swimming.

Another way of maintaining shame is self-deception in the meeting of our children's needs. Children need their parent's time and attention; it means being there for them, attending to their needs. When my children were young, I must confess I took care of my needs rather than theirs. You can watch TV while the child is in the room with you and call it "being with your child", but you are only fooling yourself. Another part of our work of love is to *listen* to our children. In America, we are trained to talk. It takes someone with maturity to listen well. If you are needy, that keeps you distracted and makes it difficult to *hear* your children. Thus they grow up without having their needs met. Underneath the mask of the adult is a needy child who never matured. That person has a hole in his soul. Thus we have so many people married to an adult child who still wants someone to mother or father them.

> You can never let someone get close to you if you feel you are flawed to the core.

Families are as sick as their secrets. You cannot solve multi-generational shame. It is kept under cover, away from the view of others. Families are ashamed of what is hidden—like suicide, incest, homosexuality, abortion, addiction, sexual abuse, financial disaster, and the list goes on and on. We cannot heal what we do not feel.[37]

Survival mechanisms like denial, idealization, repression and dissociation cause us to lose touch with our pain. This is done unconsciously on our part because these are trained responses, so we learn not to feel. A toxic shame person will marry someone, expecting to be parented. The child behind the mask requires a mother or father. This is a dysfunctional family begetting another dysfunctional family.

Here are a few of the unwritten family rules:

1 *Control* – one must be in control of all interactions, feelings and personal behavior at all times. Control is the major defense strategy for shame.

2 *Perfectionism* – always be right in everything you do. The perfectionist's rules always involve a standard which is being imposed. Fear and promotion of the negative make up the organizing principle of life. Everyone lives according to an external image; no one ever measures up.

3 *Blame* – when things don't turn out as planned, blame yourself or others. Blame is another cover-up for shame. Blame maintains the balance in a dysfunctional system when control has broken down. This was Adam's response to God, and we are good at following his example.

4 *Denial of the "five freedoms"* – The five freedoms describe full personal functionality. Each freedom has to do with a basic human power: to perceive, think and interpret; to feel; to want; to choose; and, lastly, to imagine. In shame-based families, the perfectionist rule prohibits the full expression of these powers. It says you should not perceive, think, feel, desire or imagine the way *you* do, but rather the way the perfectionist ideal demands. This takes away your opportunity to be an individual.

5 *No-talk rule* – This rule prohibits the full expression of any feeling, need or want. In shame-based families, members hide what's really going on. Therefore, no one speaks of the sense of isolation. No one can express his or her own feelings.

6 *Don't make mistakes* – Mistakes reveal the flawed, vulnerable self. To acknowledge a mistake is to open oneself to scrutiny. Cover up your own mistakes and, if someone else makes a mistake, shame him.

7 *Unreliability* – Don't expect reliability in relationships. Don't trust anyone, and you will never be disappointed. The parent did not get their developmental dependency needs met and will not be there for their child to depend on. The distrust cycle goes on.[38]

When healthy shame is transformed into toxic shame, it is called the internalization process. A feeling of healthy shame is lost, and a frozen state of being emerges. You now believe you are flawed or defective. There are three steps in this process:

Step 1 You identify with shame-based models in which you were raised.

Step 2 Your trauma of abandonment and shame binds all your feelings, needs and drives, in order to keep you from being able to express them.

Step 3 Your interconnections, and magnification of visual memories, and the retaining of shaming words are kept within yourself and never expressed.

There are three basic ways we deal with our shame:

Denial: I refuse to acknowledge my shame.

Repression: I push down my shame until I am no longer aware of it.

Transference: I shift my shame onto someone else.

As we maintain our shame, we wear our mask. We create a false self, because we believe we are flawed and worthless. We cannot look at our true self. We create a new self which is acceptable so our maintenance cycle of shame is complete.

THE SOURCES OF SHAME

CHAPTER TEN

FAMILY-BASED SHAME

Family is one part of life we have no choice about, but it deeply affects us. In the family, we are accepted, approved and loved—or we are rejected, disowned and treated with indifference. If any of the latter occurs in our life, we learn shame at an early age. Young children are not aware of what is happening to them and do not have the skills to protect themselves. So it's open season on children for shame to develop in them. In this division of the book, we will look at six basic sources that feed our shame.

1 Family
2 Society
3 Church
4 Culture
5 Corporate
6 Nation

Families shame children when they do not own them. I am not talking about slavery or ownership in that sense, but rather about the acceptance of a child and the verbal acknowledgement that, "This child is mine, he belongs, and he is my future." If the natural parents put their child up for adoption, the child experiences great shame. "Why did my parents not want me?" Meanwhile, the adoptive parents struggle to get the child to receive ownership from them. The natural soul-tie with the birth parent may keep the adopted child from bonding with the adoptive parent. Sometimes the child rejects only one of the adoptive parents—most of the time, the mother. Such children sense that if they love the adoptive mother, they must reject the birth mother. This is a deep, shameful feeling. Those who are supposed to love them did not own them, and those who have adopted them can't really connect because of the soul-ties.

Shame makes you feel you're a burden—the result of a mistake.

If you grew up in a home where the words "shame on you" were directed to the children when they stepped over the line in any area, you have no doubt experienced shame. If you had a bad grade on your report card, if you talked or misbehaved in church, if you did anything that embarrassed your parents in public, if you talked about or asked questions concerning any sexual matters, *shame on you!* That was a catchall phrase used to hammer home shame. Usually children learn quickly that when something goes wrong, they will be shamed for their lack of performance.[39]

If you grew up in a poor home, you were shamed. Your personal value was based on finances. If you were poor, you were expected to remain with the poor—never invited to visit the homes of the affluent. Or, if you did, you felt out of place because of the surroundings—and the way you were dressed. You were shamed for what you did not have.

If you grew up in a home where you were compared to your siblings, you felt shamed. "Why can't you be more like your brother?" "Why can't you make good grades like your sister?" This constant comparison makes the child feel worthless. When trouble comes, the one who is less loved is blamed. He or she always receives the largest amount of shame for any wrongdoing because they did not measure up.

You're shamed when you are born the wrong sex. Daddy wanted a son, and a little girl came along. She was never given true value. She was discounted, marked down. If the desired son comes along later, the daughter will still not feel accepted for who she is. The rejection and shame are already imbedded in her.

You may be shamed in your home if you come along unplanned. You are a late-in-life baby, and your parents never let you forget it. They did not plan for you, pray for you, or ask God for you. Shame makes you feel you're a burden—the result of a mistake.

You are shamed if you come from a broken or single-parent home. These days, divorce does not carry the stigma it did when I was a child. You were considered less than if your parents split up. This is a huge burden for a child to bear when he or she had nothing to do with the divorce. You may be looked down on by others, rejected or left out.

You're shamed when you fail to live up to the family name. Family pride may be so enormous that sometimes children are disowned, disinherited and totally rejected. A son is jailed for a criminal activity. He will never be allowed to forget the unforgivable thing he did. A family member may be charged for DUI (driving under the influence) and have his picture in the local newspaper. He receives double shame - in the family and in public.

Often people are shamed in their home if they break the accepted moral codes. A young girl finds herself pregnant, and the family makes her hang her head in shame, never letting her forget the disgrace she brought upon them. And though her baby did no wrong, it will also suffer great shame.

You may be shamed if you break from the family religion. I have friends who left their family's church and were totally disowned. Some of those families even held funerals for them, and their names were never mentioned again. I ministered to a man who was the sole heir of a prominent, wealthy family. His father was so ashamed of him leaving their church that he offered the total inheritance to each of the grandsons, one by one, if they would come back to the church and remain with him. As each one turned down grandfather's offer, his shame became yet greater, as did that of his son. Living in the family where God places us brings different challenges to each one of us, one of which is how we deal with shame.

> No family is without some form of shame, and none of the family members escapes its stain.

If you are a female, you may have grown up with shame because of male chauvinism. In the South especially, the "redneck" philosophy has reduced women to things or sex objects. In general, men all around the world have dishonored women by thinking they are superior to them, by not recognizing that they are the other half of God's image. If we are born in a home environment that teaches us to shame and be shamed, we learn to suffer in silence with it, and the family is often its biggest perpetuator. No family is without some form of shame, and none of the family members escapes its stain.

Chapter Eleven

Society-Based Shame

As we grow up and leave home, we discover that society has some very sophisticated shaming techniques. We often look down on people who are not like us. Sameness is a big deal. We all want to do the same socially acceptable things. As time goes by, society's standards change, but very slowly. So what is *in* this year may not be so a few years from now. For example, it once was unacceptable to have pre-marital sexual relationships, but now it's okay to just live together. Having an illegitimate child used to be wrong. These days, you can have a family with your significant other without ever being married. Society assigns special names for each economic group—like the "rich and famous", or the "middle class" or the "poor". In America, we do not have a caste system as does, for example, India. We do, however, have a system through which we assign shame. The further down you are in this class system, the more disgrace you encounter. Terms like, "I was born on the wrong side of the tracks," indicate that you have been shamed. Society will make sure you own that classification. We ask questions like, "What does your father do?" or, "What is your family business?" According to your answer, you will receive more or less humiliation.

Many pre-teens and teen-agers never invite anyone to their home because they are ashamed of where they live. They never want to offer someone a ride because of the car the family has. You will, most likely, not find the teacher's pet being a dumb, ugly girl, because only the talented and the gifted get those breaks. A plain girl from a low-income family feels shamed, left out and overlooked. Many teenage girls attempt suicide because they are not accepted in the *right* group or club at school, which brings humiliation.

Society shows no mercy when it comes to shame. We live in a crazy world which demands we must be a "10". Most American women today walk around feeling inferior because they don't measure up to the ideal. Pornographic images have shown us what a "10" looks like. Only a small percentage of the women in America meet the Playboy model stats. This is why we have an epidemic of teens and twenty-something's having breast augmentation surgeries. They are not satisfied with the way God made them. They need to be a "10" so they don't feel shame.

> Society shows no mercy when it comes to shame.

When we have nine out of ten people who are not happy about how they look, we are in trouble. Their nose is too big or not big enough. Their lips are not the right size or shape. Their ears stick out too much. In other words, they are not perfect. Young girls play with the Barbie doll, which has caused them to focus on their outward appearance. "Barbie was a '10' in every way, so I must be, too!" Dolls *can* be made perfect, but human beings are created with qualities unique to themselves.

Men too feel they must be a "10". This is why we go to such great lengths to use steroids to build our bodies and have all kinds of surgeries done to enhance our manliness. We are just as vain as women and will do similar things to reach the "10". We get face-lifts, dye our hair, transplant hair, wear wigs and toupees. Men who are bald on top but have hair on the sides will let the sides grow very long and comb it over the bald spot. Everyone else may think it looks rather ridiculous, but they act like no one knows.

You will encounter truckloads of shame if you are not a "man's man". You're made fun of and laughed at. To avoid this, you must be able to work on cars, do all kinds of home repairs, paint the house, groom the lawn and defend your household. If you can't do all of these things well, you are made to feel less than a man. Many of us have had to find a technical excuse to call a plumber or an electrician because we had no idea how to solve the problem when we started. Once we start, we can't stop because of shame. "I must accomplish this job if I am going to be a man." But, in reality, being able to do repairs is more a matter of training than gender.

Our society does not handle emotions very well. We learn rituals of acting happy and being fine at a very early age. We ask people all the time, "How are you doing today? How are things with you?" They have learned to respond from the mask that they wear saying, "I'm fine. I'm good. I'm doing well. I am blessed." If someone breaks that rule, we shame him or her by saying, "Nobody wants to hear your problems. Suck it up, and smile. You'll be all right." Emotions are not acceptable in the workplace. If you don't learn to smile, you may lose your job, and more shame will come your way.

Our nation does not want a leader who expresses sadness and emotion. Remember Senator Edmund Muskie who was running for president? On the campaign trail, he broke down and cried. His emotional outburst was broadcast on national news, and he was "history" from that time on. We want a president who can *act* strong and be strong, not one who displays emotions. We're taught to be nice and polite. Those behaviors, which most of the time are lies, seem better than telling the truth. Our churches, schools, homes and political arenas are rampant with these teachings of dishonesty. You meet a person who is sick and has a high fever; yet he says, "I'm fine!" Everyone can see he's sick, but he has been taught to always confess the positive and not the negative. That man will lie about how he really feels, because he does not want to be shamed.

> We have unwritten laws in our society which we are expected to obey.

We say things we don't mean. We smile when we are sad and laugh nervously when dealing with grief. We roar at jokes we don't think are funny and tell people things we don't mean. Playing a role and acting are forms of lying. If a person acts as he really feels and tells it like it is, he is ostracized. We have unwritten laws in our society which we are expected to obey, and we are deeply shamed if we rebel against them.

CHAPTER TWELVE

CHURCH-BASED SHAME

Going to church should be an uplifting experience. However, in many cases, you come away feeling depressed and shamed. Many churches place their greatest emphasis on how we have failed to please God. Christianity has become a performance rather than a relationship for many. You must try harder, do more, and be more dedicated than ever before. Unfortunately, early in my 45-year ministry, I fell into this trap. On Sunday as people left the service, they would often say, "Pastor, you sure did step on my toes today." Foolishly, I thought that meant I had succeeded because I had made them feel guilty. Such doctrines and teachings cause the negative to stand tall and strong—we are forced to focus on our failures, rather than on encouragement from a God who has forgiven all our sins and loves us with His whole heart. God is not trying to hurt us, He is trying to heal us and make us whole.

You can't foster a deeper relationship with God by picturing Him as Heaven's Chief of Police walking around with His billy-club, hitting you on the head every time your performance is not one hundred percent. This is not the God of the Bible. God is love; God is forgiveness and grace. That is the whole point of the cross. We couldn't perform! Sadly we have often made the church a major place of shame for the believer. But, if I understand Scripture correctly, when God forgives my sins, he puts them away from me "as far as the east is from the west". I am glad He did not say "as far as the north is from the south". The distance of east from west is infinite. If you got on an airplane today and began to fly east, you could continue for the rest of your life and never be flying west, and vice versa. But, going north, as soon as you passed over the North Pole, you would be heading south and, after approximately 17,000 miles, you would cross over the South Pole and be flying north again. I thank God that His word assures me my sins are forgiven and as far from me as infinity!

> As far as the east is from the west, So far has He removed our transgressions from us. (Psalm 103:12)

If that is reality, why do I still view myself as a sinner? As a young Christian, I was taught that I was a sinner saved by grace. Yes, I was a sinner but, by God's grace through the blood of the Lamb, I am no longer guilty.

> Therefore, if anyone is in Christ, he is a new creation; old things have passed away; behold, all things have become new. (2 Corinthians 5:17)

If I am a new creation in Christ, I am now an heir of God. I am a new person in Christ. I have a new identity. No doubt, I will slip and sin along the way but, if I *think* I am a sinner, I do not yet understand that my identity has changed. The people of God often are covered with shrouds of toxic shame, because we do not change our view of who we are.

So many Christians today still struggle with some form of bondage. Others walk in discouragement and guilt because they do not *do* enough. As a child in church, I learned to lie to avoid the shame of failure in my performance. Each child in the Sunday school would receive an envelope with a number of little boxes to check off things you had done that week and, of course, to put your offering in. One of those boxes was daily Bible reading. I tried to read every day, but some times it just did not work out. The teacher would ask us to raise our hands as he read the check-list. Rather than feel the condemnation, I would raise my hand along with the other children. I learned a "performance relationship" with God at a very early age, with no hope of ever measuring up to the standard.

As I listened to the pastor preach, I would receive more shame, especially

> God is not trying to hurt us, He is trying to heal us and make us whole.

in the area of witnessing. I can still hear these words ringing in my ear: "If you have not won someone to Jesus this week, why are you still alive?" Eventually you learn to harden your heart, tune out those shaming words and go on with life. God wants us to walk in grace.

We bring shame on other believers by our judgmental attitudes about their performance or lack of performance.[40] In the church, we often judge out of fear that we might fall into sin or error. Yet we're urged not to judge.

> "Judge not, that you be not judged. For with what judgment you judge, you will be judged; and with the measure you use, it will be measured back to you." (Matthew 7:1-2)

Judgments toward others come from our feelings of haughtiness and pride. However, these attitudes are sometimes just a cover-up. We often lift ourselves up above other people trying to make ourselves feel better. We need to remember that we are all of inestimable value in God's sight. When we pass judgment, we shame a brother or sister in Christ. It makes them feel like failures. But the blood of Jesus covers all failure and sin – theirs and ours.

> There is therefore now no condemnation to those who are in Christ Jesus, who do not walk according to the flesh, but according to the Spirit. (Romans 8:1)

If God does not consider them condemned, how can I? We all need to remember Paul's admonition.

> Therefore let him who thinks he stands take heed lest he fall. (1 Corinthians 10:12)

Another great source of shame in the church is divorce. It has become less disgraceful in some circles but, in most conservative groups, it is still the great disqualifier. In many circles, you cannot become a pastor if you are divorced. And if you are a pastor and get divorced, you lose that privilege. You become a second-class member of the church. You cannot be a deacon or a Sunday school teacher—or hold a leadership office in the church.

Most divorced women who remain single are looked down on and shamed sexually. They are thought of as willing sexual partners for those who want to be immoral. They are accused of having lower moral standards or no moral standards. Many are shamed without cause. This is wrong. I cannot find, in Scripture that divorce is the unpardonable sin. Yet those who have suffered through it receive great humiliation—being looked down upon and sometimes even shunned. They do not deserve this kind of shame. The church stamps the big "D" over their life. Yes, God hates divorce (and I hate divorce), but He loves people who are divorced, as do I. God's callings and gifts were not suddenly withdrawn when this tragedy happened.

> For the gifts and the calling of God are irrevocable. (Romans 11:29)

So if God has ever called a person, he or she is still called, and if He has ever gifted a person, the gifts remain. Either Jesus has died for all of our sins, or none of them are forgiven. Thank God for His incredible love for each of us.

> Either Jesus has died for all of our sins, or none of them are forgiven.

Another area where churches may point the finger is toward those who struggle with addictions. It is so easy to play the hypocrite and shame them, while we are addicted in another area. The obese pastor shames a man who struggles with alcohol or sex addiction. Yes, drunkenness and immorality are sin and should not happen in the life of a believer. Gluttony is also a sin. Whatever your addiction is, God wants you to deal with it. Some are more acceptable to the church than others. For example, it is okay to be a workaholic. But is workaholism a good thing? It keeps us from vital relationships - with our spouse, our children and the body of Christ. We place differing amounts and degrees of shame on others, according to our opinion of the addiction. Pride and arrogance keep us judging them while we are ensnared by something that's considered okay.

Shame also shows up in the life of the affluent. I remember, many years ago we had just dedicated a new educational building at the church I pastored. We also ran bus routes to pick up the poor and misfortunate children in our city. A wealthy lady said to me one day, "We gave a lot of money for this to be built, and we don't want to ruin this beautiful place with these dirty kids from across town. I am ashamed to bring my friends here." It is true that many churches are ashamed of the poor and needy who come. But church should be the place we can come to be free from shame, not to receive it.

CHAPTER THIRTEEN

CULTURE-BASED SHAME

The cultures of the world have different shame structures, but they all hold people in shame. When I was a child, I did not want anyone to know that I was descended from a Native American ancestor. I have some Cherokee through my mother's side of the family. Her major bloodline was Irish, so that was acceptable. But many people made shameful, hurtful remarks about Indians. I never heard about their strengths, only their weaknesses. "Indians are lazy. All they do is sit around on the reservation and gamble and drink. You can't trust them. They are a bunch of no-good thieves." If someone gave you something and then wanted it back, they were called an "Indian giver". It was known that most Indians could not hold their liquor, so they were easy targets for alcoholism. It was often said, "A good Irishman can drink an Indian into the ground any day of the week." When I became an adult, I learned about all the immorality that took place on the reservations, and that brought more humiliation on me. I never felt free to acknowledge my heritage until I was just past forty years old. I lived in shame because of my ancestry.

ETHNIC SHAME

I grew up in North Louisiana. As a child, I was taught that black people were inferior. Some of my ancestors were slave owners, and I was trained in prejudice early on. I grew up on a farm where our closest neighbors were black families. Before I started going to school, some of my playmates were black children. I went to a totally white school, so I had no black playmates there. We had a black family who worked for us and became very close to us.

> If I don't know my true identity, I am an easy target for shame to manipulate me.

J. C. and Vermer and their seven children became good friends; yet I never understood why they had to enter our house through the back door when my family came through their front door. To me, there was something basically wrong about this, and I felt shame. Even when blacks came to a white church (if they were allowed to come in at all), they were allowed to sit only on the back row. When we visited a black church, we sat in a special section designated for white people. All of this seemed shameful to me. It took God many years to deal with my prejudice and shame concerning my black brothers and sisters.

I became a Boy Scout, and our troop held a place of honor in our town. One day, the Harlem Globe Trotters came to our school to play basketball and to showcase their abilities as athletes. The Scouts were given the privilege of escorting these men and seeing that their needs were met. One of them asked if he could go to a restaurant because he was hungry. I took him to the front door of the only restaurant in our town. He was met by the owner and told he had to come through the back door and be served where the colored people ate. I was totally shocked at how the owner humiliated this man. That memory remained with me for a number of years. Today, young black men are looked down on and shamed. Three out of four black males will be in jail at some time in their lives. This brings great shame to those who desire to follow after God and those who become good citizens. They are judged for things they have never done. Another shaming technique of our society is to call a black man "Boy". We hear racial slurs and bigotry all the time. These are statements of shame.

We hear of other races and groups being treated similarly. All of the "Polack" jokes are attempts to make fun of the Polish people. The Jewish slurs are more of the same. You are as "tight as a Jew." You need to "Jew him down," because he is asking too much money for his merchandise. These are statements that put shame on a person because he is of another race or nation. Unhealed, generational shame has affected our entire culture.[41]

The need for white men to feel superior to other races is what has kept the Ku Klux Klan and similar organizations alive and allowed shame to be passed down from generation to generation. We have brought shame on some of our finest citizens, because we can't get free from our own shame.

GENDER SHAME

The workplace has brought shame to women. Even today, employers, if they can get by with it, will pay a man more per hour than a woman. Only in the last few years have most work areas been opened up to women. For many years, only men were medical doctors. Now, women are accepted in this field, but I still hear women who go to medical school say, "I have to work twice as hard as the men to get the same grade, to prove that I am capable of being a doctor." Women are laughed at, scorned and shamed for attempting to break into a male-dominated career. It is a medical and scientific fact that women typically do not have the same upper body strength as men. So, I believe some jobs should be reserved for men, in order to spare women the abuse. This is not shame speaking, but common sense.

CLASS SHAME

Cultural shame causes a person with a low income to spend money on clothes, shoes, shirts, etc., so they can appear wealthier than they are. Poverty can be a mindset and an attitude, rather than just a condition. As I travel across the U.S. and the world, I meet people trying to impress others that they have more than they really do. This is shame driving them. Today, we have an epidemic of people declaring they have graduated from a college they never attended. You cannot trust some to fill out their employment applications honestly. We have others saying they have received certain military honors, like the Purple Heart, when it's not true.

If I don't know my true identity, I am an easy target for shame to manipulate me. I may make false statements about my self-worth and claim achievements I have never accomplished. Cultural shame is no new thing. We should ask God to show us how to remove it from our society and our culture.

CHAPTER FOURTEEN

CORPORATE-BASED SHAME

Madison Avenue has discovered that man can be motivated by shame to buy products he does not have or need. Advertising fuels our economy. It is what we don't have that triggers disgrace. Many times we don't even realize that shame is a part of our life. The old saying, "He who dies with the most toys wins" is a shame-based statement. Our desire not to lose keeps us buying and buying. What the statement forgets to say is, "He who dies with the most toys is still dead." The need to perform to prove ourselves always comes from the sense of lack.[42]

If you keep listening to Madison Avenue advertisers, they will show you something you do not have or something you must have. "If you buy this wrinkle cream, you will always look young." This advertisement appeals to the shame of aging. The car industry has learned to motivate you to buy their car rather than the competitor's. "Our car goes faster, uses less gasoline, is more comfortable, and you can qualify to buy no matter what your credit score." These car ads may have as a spokesperson some gorgeous, sexy woman, almost convincing you that she comes with the car.

It does not matter what the product is. The advertising world appeals to the shame of what we do not have. Women have kitchen cabinets and clothes closets full of items they "could not live without", and most men have a garage full of stuff they have never used or will never use again. "If I don't have one of *these*, I'm a nobody. Since I can't stand being a nobody, I have to buy again. I will never use this thing, but I have to get one so that I can be a somebody." You have been lied to and motivated by shame. Most advertising enforces the mask that we wear. We must keep our mask in place because we have become comfortable with our false self.

We hear statements like "Where did you buy that shirt or blouse?" If your answer is, "Wal-Mart," you're looked at with contempt. This is especially true of teenagers of the moneyed class. The affluent somehow gauge their worth on where they buy their clothes and other things. The statement, "Clothes make the man" is not true; it is shame-driven. Character cannot be changed or improved by exclusive designer labels and expensive prices. Being driven by what we do not have may cause one teenager to kill another for his jacket or tennis shoes.

> The need to perform to prove ourselves always comes from the sense of lack.

We have placed so much of our value on how we look, what brand names we wear, where we bought it and how much we paid. If we can't get all these things, we come to the conclusion we are of no value, and no one will receive us into their inner circle.

Here is another shame-maker. "What college did you graduate from?" If you graduated from one of the few Ivy League colleges, you are considered to have gotten the best education our nation can offer. On the other hand, if you started at a community college and then graduated from some small state college, shame on you. (And *double shame* if you did not go to college at all.)

The wife who pushes her husband to buy a bigger house and keep up with the Jones' is an example of a person with a shame-based philosophy driven to buy to prove their worth. Just remember, every time you think you have caught up with the Jones', they just refinance and buy again, and you are left behind. It is a never-ending cycle of slavery. When will enough be enough? Jesus said that our life is not about having the most toys.

And He said to them, "Take heed and beware of covetousness, for one's life does not consist in the abundance of the things he possesses." (Luke 12:15)

CHAPTER FIFTEEN

NATIONAL-BASED SHAME

Shame can come upon a country through war, national sins, abuse of power, etc. We don't think much about the shame of our nation, because most of us have never done anything to bring shame to it. In our country's early years, we brought disgrace on ourselves by how we dealt with the Native Americans—the Indians. Many believed they were without a soul. They were just wild beasts to be hunted down and killed. This was nothing more than ethnic cleansing. Our nation signed hundreds of peace agreements and treaties with different Indian nations, but all of them were broken. It seemed the United States Government had no intention of keeping their end of the bargain. Thus, the white man became known as "one who speaks with forked tongue", or one who lies.

> A heart that devises wicked plans, feet that are swift in running to evil, a false witness who speaks lies, and one who sows discord among brethren. (Proverbs 6:18-19)

> Righteousness exalts a nation, but sin is a reproach to any people. (Proverbs 14:34)

Americans have fought numerous wars, but one war in particular was different and still holds our nation in its grip. This war divided family against family and brother against brother. The southern states were defeated by the northern states, but the shame has never left to this day. Being raised in the South, I have often heard our fellow Americans from the northern states referred to as those "damn Yankees". This was not a term of endearment but rather one of anger. The shame of defeat caused the men in grey to return home with condemnation. Because of this, there are still strongholds of rebellion in the Southland. Shame does not allow a man to save face and keep his honor. We have those who still honor the rebel flag and save their Confederate money, believing the South will rise again so they can be free from the shame that drives them. Our nation has never really been healed of its deep wounds. When Southerners go north, they often feel the shame of being from the South. I'm sure it's the same for Northerners when they go south. Shame leaves an ugly stain on our soul.

Shame can come through being a part of certain ethnic groups. After World War II, if you were of German heritage, you were shamed for the murderous actions of Adolf Hitler. He and the nation of Germany became synonymous. The swastika, the emblem of Hitler's Nazi Party, was one of great shame. It symbolized hate, especially for Jews and blacks. Consequently, hatred for Germans ran so deep that many of them were killed, even though they had not followed the evil dictator.

> Shame leaves an ugly stain on our soul.

When the wicked comes, contempt comes also; and with dishonor comes reproach. (Proverbs 18:3)

As World War II drew to a close, Japan was bombed, and many Japanese people (who had come to the U.S. before the war began) found themselves being deeply shamed. They were hunted down like wild animals and confined in concentration camps just because they were Japanese. Out of shame came many ethnic slurs: terms like "Japs", "slant-eyes", "Nips", "slopes", "beady-eyes", etc. All these terms brought humiliation to the Japanese people but were born out of our national pride.

The Jewish people have suffered from shame down through the centuries. America turned them away at our harbors as they sought refuge. We have looked down on and disdained them for their values and way of life. We have developed a number of ethnic slurs. We have repressed, disrespected, isolated and shamed Jewish people in America.

We are becoming a nation of "haves" and "have-nots". The "haves" are beginning to bring shame on the "have-nots". People from the inner city are being rejected and despised. What little chance they have to escape their miserable life is being taken away. We are ashamed of the poor people, the projects and the inner-city child. We often are not as open, loving and kind, respectful and encouraging to that child as we are to an upper class child. Why? Because we're ashamed of how they dress and behave and of the stereotyping we have created toward them. Shame causes us to turn a deaf ear to their pain and cries. It keeps us from opening our heart to their needs.

> We have put a man on the Moon and landed equipment on Mars, but we cannot take away our shame.

Great shame was brought on the city of Dallas, Texas, when President John F. Kennedy was shot and killed. I remember exactly where I was when it happened. I was eating lunch at home and watching the noon news. The flash came, "President Kennedy has been shot." To this day, Dallas has never lived down the shame of that event. The Dallas Police Department did not protect our President, and they were blamed for it. Our entire nation suffered that day and we are still feeling its effects.

Our nation has also experienced shame because of the violence, sexual abuse, and injustices that have happened in America. Terrible disgrace came as a result of opposition to the Civil Rights movement and the inequity which many in the black community suffered because of it. Shame has come to the U.S. from being the pornography capital of the world. We may have put a man on the Moon and landed equipment on Mars, but somehow we cannot take away our shame. It is a tragedy that our society is still reaching out to destroy itself.

We have dumped loads of shame on our Vietnam War veterans. The young men and women went off to fight for an oppressed nation and, when they returned, our nation rejected them. Many of them were deeply wounded when they came home and their families rejected them. Many were cursed and spit upon. They were called "women- killers", "child-killers" and the like. No other war veterans have been treated the way these men were. This war brought shame to our nation. We did not win. We had nothing to show for all of the thousands who gave their lives. It is said that Buddhist monks put a curse on our soldiers, and no one has taken it away. They were cursed to be wanderers, homeless, isolated and to die alone. But, there is hope. The curse can be broken and the shame can be removed.

As a result of the Watergate conspiracy, President Richard Nixon was forced to resign because of his wrongdoing. It mattered not whether you were Democrat, Republican or Independent. We all suffered disgrace. We could go on and on about how the deeds of others have brought shame on us.

By the blessing of the upright the city is exalted, but it is overthrown by the mouth of the wicked. (Proverbs 11:11)

We have tried to lift our head high. America has been a leader in the world, but the shame of our national sins has deeply stained us as a people.

THE ANSWER TO SHAME

Chapter Sixteen

Shame and Grace

Most of us are familiar with shame, but somehow we have failed to get a clear view of grace. We often confuse our roles in life with our true self. When we identify ourselves by our accomplishments, we bring more shame into our lives. To rid ourselves of it, we must ask, "Why is shame such a heavy load for the human spirit to carry? How does it get such power to rob us of the joy of living?"

Until we **experience** the grace of God, we can never feel accepted. Rejection always keeps us on the outside looking in. God's grace means He has forgiven *all* our sins and accepted us as we are—warts and all! So we must **experience** God's grace to begin our journey to healing and wholeness. To try to explain what it took for God to extend His wonderful gift is nearly impossible. There are four ways most people receive it:

1 We experience grace as pardon. We are forgiven for wrongs we have done. Pardon relieves us of guilt.

2 We experience grace as acceptance. We are reunited to God in our true self—cradled, held, affirmed and loved. Acceptance is the answer to shame.

3 We experience grace as power. It provides spiritual energy to shed the heaviness of shame and move us toward the true self God meant us to be.

4 We experience grace as gratitude. It gives us a sense for the gift of life, a sense of wonder and sometimes elation at the lavish generosity of God. Gratitude is the grace for thankfulness.[43]

Let's examine grace as acceptance. Not being accepted allows shame to come to us, while being accepted removes it. The best cure for feeling unacceptable is discovering we are received by the grace of the One whose acceptance matters most. Shame will rob you of your childhood, but grace will give it back to you. Often a child comes into this world, and the parents, especially the father, do not own or receive the child as an extension of themselves. Perhaps the child was not really wanted, or it may have been conceived illegitimately, born at the wrong time or born the wrong sex. For whatever reason, the father does not claim the child as his own. Though it struggles to do so, the child never receives a sense of belonging. Shame comes immediately into the spirit of that child, and the enemy plants the lie, "You are a mistake!" From then on, the child's life may run increasingly downhill. If it is a female, she may always be trying to win the approval of men, making numerous wrong decisions in her life trying to get that approval.[44]

> We must **experience** God's grace to begin our journey to healing and wholeness.

I ministered to a woman in her sixties. Alice had been in two relationships with men who controlled, used and blamed her. Her first husband got her to give in to him sexually before they were married. She met all his demands because she needed someone to claim her, to call her his very own, but she never experienced that acceptance. This same need kept her in a second abusive marriage for 12 years. She put up with all of this, until I led her to accept her heavenly Father as her true "Daddy". When she experienced the ownership of God, she broke free from shame and the hunger for approval by others. She is still walking in the freedom that grace gives. She said to me, "There is a wonderful weightlessness in grace. I don't feel heavy anymore."

RACEHOSS SAMPLE

People can accept a measure of the grace of God in their life and yet never let go of shame. Therefore, they can never be transformed. I want to tell you the stories of two men that illustrate the power of grace. One is of Racehoss Sample, and the other is of C. Prescott McCaernish from Lewis Smede's book, *Shame and Grace*. Racehoss was a son of Big Emma, a prostitute who made her living by providing gambling and bootleg whiskey along with the sex she sold in a shack near a railroad stop in the middle of Texas. Racehoss got in Big Emma's way, and she resented him for it from the start. She beat him whenever she was drunk, which was a great deal of the time, and she let him know he was *less* than worthless. When he turned eleven years old, Racehoss could not stand it anymore, and he took off. He ran away to nowhere special, riding the rails wherever they took him, hanging out with bums and hoboes along the way. He became a creature of volcanic rage. World War II broke out, and the U.S. Army drafted him but soon discovered they could not tame him. He went absent without leave (AWOL) every month or so and, each time, he got into a fight and was sent to jail for assault and battery. Finally, they sentenced him to thirty years in the Texas penitentiary where he learned that, if you treat a person like an animal, he becomes one. The worst punishment they had for untamable prisoners was confinement in the "tomb". The tomb was actually a four-by-eight-foot basement cell with no windows, two solid steel plates for a door and a concrete slab for a bed and a large open hole in the floor to pass for a toilet. The stench lingered from one occupant to the next. This is where they stuck any prisoner who forgot to grovel in front of his white boss. They locked him in there for 28 days—with a cup of water and one biscuit a day, and one meal of mush every six days to keep him alive. Racehoss spent a considerable amount of time there. In the sixteenth year of his captivity, he contradicted one of the guards and was locked in again, but this time it was not the same. He heard a sound of rushing water nearby, and he knew for sure it was going to come in and drown him. He went crazy. He tried climbing the walls and then rolled on the floor like a ball. He mauled himself, tore his body and slumped exhausted on the slab. He covered his face with both hands and cried out, "Help me, God, help me!" Then a ray of light between his fingers began to shine on his face. The tomb was illuminated as if a 100-watt bulb had been turned on. The light soothed him, and he was no longer afraid.

> Shame will rob you of your childhood, but grace will give it back to you.

Engulfed by a presence, he felt reassured and comforted. He breathed deeply and peacefully. He had never felt so good in all his life. He sensed safety and love. A voice within talked through the pit of his belly: "You're not an animal; you're a human being. Don't worry about a thing, but you must tell them about Me." After that, God was real. Racehoss testified, "He found me in the abyss of the burning hell, uplifted and fed my hungry soul and breathed new life into my nostrils." When they let him out, the authorities weighed him and noted he had gained five pounds. The way God came to Racehoss Sample may not be His normal way to the human soul. Nonetheless, what he experienced, when God came, was pure grace. The only message Racehoss got was what he had ached to hear just once from Big Emma, and now he heard it from God, "You are accepted."

What was the result of such easygoing grace, which accepted a sinner and demanded nothing more than that he tell people about the One whom he met in the tomb? A great deal actually. Racehoss walked out of prison on January 12, 1972, at 9:45am with $10.00 in his pocket. Later on, he wrote his memoirs. But we find elsewhere he was the first ex-convict ever to work in the Governor's office, the first to serve as a probation officer, and the first to serve on the Texas state bar as a division head. He changed his name to Alfred Sample in 1976. He received a full pardon, was given the Liberty Bell award and named the outstanding crime prevention citizen of Texas in 1981. His story is a testimony to the truth that grace can completely transform a shamed person's life.

C. Prescott McCaernish

Now comes the story of C. Prescott McCaernish, the son of a minister of the Gospel. The message from the beginning was, "Your father is a great man of God. If you can be half the man he is, you will do well." He heard it from his mother and everyone around him. He never forgot. So C. Prescott devoted himself to the kind of life that would make him acceptable in the eyes of God and his father. The first thing he needed was a call to be a minister. By the time he was 45 years old, every Sunday morning, in a flowing blue gown, he preached three splendid sermons to more than two thousand believers.

Was he "half the man"? To ninety-five percent of the world, he was more than his father was. And the other five percent? He gave them more, and then some more. He was available to everyone who needed counsel. He would turn a young woman's wedding into a pageant. He became a delegate to his denomination's national assembly, willing to run for the high office, if necessary, whatever it took. But on the inside, C. Prescott McCaernish was a frightened child, ashamed that he could never be the man his father was. He met someone who had a talent for accepting unacceptable men. She nestled him, warmed him, excited him, and accepted him. She took him in—and the congregation put him out. Here lies C. Prescott McCaernish, a casualty of "Virtual Unacceptable Syndrome". He had grace in the palm of his hand, but he could never close his fingers around it and take it to his lips. He worked in the atmosphere of grace but breathed the smog of shame. Grace genuinely experienced is not really dangerous at all. What is dangerous is the wearisome, joy killing heaviness of living without grace.[45]

> If you embrace His grace, it will transform you into a person with purpose and a destiny.

How do we find our way to peace in this life? We must understand that it really was God who planned our introduction to this world. He formed us in our mother's womb. God uses women and men for the raw materials, but He is the one who creates people and life. You were with God in Heaven, and one day He said, "I need someone to go to earth for me." God placed your spirit in a newly-formed person in a woman's womb, and nine months later you and your body were born. Your earthly father or parents may not have wanted you, but your real Father always has. If we suffer from the hurts, pain, rejection, abandonment and abuse of earthly parents and others, we feel and believe what these experiences tell us. Though you were too young to understand, when bad things happened, God never did any of these things to you. You didn't know who your real Father was. The only way to take away your shame is to know the truth that God's grace is available to you.[46] It will put shame to flight. Shame can no longer be a part of your life. If you embrace His grace, it will transform you into a person with purpose and a destiny. If you reject it, you will stumble along in life, believing the experiences you have are the ultimate truth. God has called us to believe and know the Truth, and it will set us free.

I was talking with James a few days ago. He was relating to me how, in his whole life, his father never gave him one compliment. Dad always looked at the negative. Everything was not good enough, not right, not acceptable. When James graduated from high school at the age of 17, he moved away from home to go to college. He set out to prove that he was worth something. His father did not approve of the woman he chose to marry, because of how her family had behaved themselves in the community in the past, and he said to him, "This is the wrong choice, and you will regret this as long as you live." James had an extremely sensitive spirit. Therefore, he turned all this criticism inward which drove him into a life of pain and agony striving to prove himself. He became a successful man in many areas, but he never won his father's approval. It was always, "You can do better. You can do more."

James never experienced the grace and power of accomplishment and acceptance. He always suffered the shame of defeat, believing he was unacceptable. James is now an old man; his dad is dead and gone. But he is still driven by the lack of ownership of his father. James still hears his words, "You did not do this right. You're unacceptable. Your life is a mess. You will never make right decisions." How will James ever turn this around? How will he ever become acceptable in his own sight? He must experience God's ownership. He made him; He loves him and approves of him. James was nearly fifty years old before he accepted Jesus. His father and mother were very religious people. Therefore, he could not understand how God, who said He loved him, could allow him to be treated the way he was. James didn't know the grace of God, but he will in time, and his life will be transformed as are hundreds of others by simply knowing **experientially** that we may not be acceptable to other humans, but God receives us as "accepted in the beloved." That is what grace is all about.

CHAPTER SEVENTEEN

OTHER FACETS OF SHAME

Scripture says Jesus bore our sins and set us free, but he refused the shame that was brought to Him on the cross.

> Looking unto Jesus, the author and finisher of our faith, who for the joy that was set before Him endured the cross, despising the shame, and has sat down at the right hand of the throne of God. (Hebrews 12:2)

The word "despised" in this passage means "not to receive". The Greek word *kataphroneo* means to "think down upon or against anyone". Jesus refused to receive the shame that Satan tried to put on Him. He hung naked and scorned on the cross, but He did not receive the shame of that exposure. Jesus was on the cross out of obedience, and His obedience was a blessing. It was our disgrace He bore, not His own. We too can reject toxic shame. However, if we walk in disobedience, it will come upon us. Shame will always present itself after our disobedience.[47] If Jesus is our example in life, we do not have to receive shame.

> The Lord GOD has opened my ear; And I was not rebellious, Nor did I turn away. I gave My back to those who struck Me, And My cheeks to those who plucked out the beard; I did not hide My face from shame and spitting. For the Lord GOD will help Me; Therefore I will not be

disgraced; Therefore I have set My face like a flint, And I know that I
will not be ashamed. (Isaiah 50:5-7)

We can face shame and not embrace it. We have the power to reject
toxic shame. When we experience something we consider shameful, we are
tempted to internalize it. If we allow this to happen, it
means we have not dealt with our past shame. If we are
free from that, then we can resist receiving future shame.
Those of us who have had shame-based personalities
always want to help everyone in need and rescue those
caught in shame.[48] One reason we do this is to spare them from going
through more painful experiences. Because Jesus knew His identity in the
Father, He refused to accept the lies of the enemy. He is showing us that we
too can refuse shame if we know our identity is in Him.

Shame will always present itself after our disobedience.

Hope is an essential part of overcoming shame.

Now hope does not make ashamed, because the love of God has
been poured out in our hearts by the Holy Spirit who was given to us.
(Romans 5:5)

The reason hope is so important is because it is the foundation on which
our faith rests. Our hope is in Jesus. He will take our shame if we release
ourselves to Him.

To You, O LORD, I lift up my soul.
O my God, I trust in You;
Let me not be ashamed;
Let not my enemies triumph over me.
Indeed, let no one who waits on You be ashamed;
Let those be ashamed who deal treacherously without cause.
Show me Your ways, O LORD;
Teach me Your paths. (Psalm 25:1-4)

If I trust in God, I will not be brought to shame; I will wait on God to work
it out. How long? As long as it takes. This is not a short-term battle. I will
stand fast in Jesus. Hope will disarm shame in my life.

Remember the word to your servant , upon which you have caused me
to hope. (Psalm 119:49)

Just one word from God, written or spoken, can take away our shame
because it gives us hope. Every prophetic word is one of hope.

"Man does not live by bread alone but by every word that proceeds
from the mouth of God." (Matthew 4:4)

There is nothing like a word from the Father to create hope in our spirit.[49]

Uphold me according to your word, that I may live; and do not let me
be ashamed of my hope. (Psalm 119:116)

Like nothing else, God speaking to us brings hope. It brings life, where life
is slipping away. It builds us up in our spiritual man, so
we are not afraid. Our hope is in what God says and
does for us.

> We can face
> shame and not
> embrace it.

In Scripture many different attitudes and behaviors
are related to shame. Poverty and shame are often
connected together. The person who will not take
instructions will also come to shame.

Poverty and shame will come to him who disdains correction, But he
who regards a rebuke will be honored. (Proverbs 13:18)

Did you realize that the root of shame is pride? We elevate our own
thoughts, experiences and ideas above what God says.

When pride comes, then comes shame; But with the humble is
wisdom. (Proverbs 11:2)

Our pride often causes us to answer in the midst of another's question
or statement, without waiting to hear the whole matter. It is pride that brings
us to shame.

He who answers a matter before he hears it, It is folly and shame to
him. (Proverbs 18:13)

True humility is the forgetting of oneself, but shame comes as you focus on yourself. The humble heart will focus on others.

Our hidden shame will cause us to lie, which will bring yet more shame into our lives.

> A righteous man hates lying, But a wicked man is loathsome and comes to shame. (Proverbs 13:5)

Sometimes, demonically influenced people try to shame us. We must resist the onslaught of the enemy but also realize our battle is not with the person. We're at war with the forces of darkness.

> For we do not wrestle against flesh and blood, but against principalities, against powers, against the rulers of the darkness of this age, against spiritual hosts of wickedness in the heavenly places. (Ephesians 6:12)

How do we deal with those who oppose us?

> Do not let me be ashamed, O LORD, for I have called upon You; Let the wicked be ashamed; Let them be silent in the grave. (Psalm 31:17)

The wicked, not the believer, will be brought to shame. We should cry out to Father God to protect us and fight for us. Toxic shame has no place in the heart or life of His child.

> Let those be put to shame and brought to dishonor who seek after my life; Let those be turned back and brought to confusion who plot my hurt. (Psalm 35:4)

We need to use the prayer in Psalm 35:1-8, asking God to fight against our enemies. We do not need to seek revenge. We must leave that up to Him. If we walk upright before God and obey Him, He will bring justice in our lives. We don't have to take matters in our own hands. God is quite capable. He takes seriously those who seek to deride, humiliate and shame His children.

> Let them be ashamed and brought to mutual confusion who seek to destroy my life; let them be driven backward and brought to dishonor

who wish me evil. Let them be confounded because of their shame, who say to me, "Aha, aha!" (Psalm 40:14-15)

Our walk with God must be with a pure heart. We must not desire harm for others, nor desire to see evil returned for evil on others, even our enemies. Our prayer is for God to perform justice, however He may choose. When we look to God, we see His provision for us. When we look to ourselves, we see what we don't have, and we are filled with shame. Our self-appraisal must always match God's appraisal of us, or we will fall for the lies Satan tells us. Jesus is our model for relationship with the Father. Jesus never worried about what man thought or did because of His relationship with God. As we develop our relationship with Him, we, too, can come to a place where what others think, say or do does not disturb our peace. The thieves crucified with Jesus are good examples of the ways we can handle shame in our lives. The first thief put Jesus down, accused him and died in his shame. The other one humbled himself, repented of his sins, gave himself to Jesus and died free from his shame.

> We must dislodge the lies that are obstacles to freedom.

If you are aware that you have been a shame-based person, how do you begin to change? The initial step is to recognize the strongholds in our minds and emotions. They form a fortress of self-protection, which becomes a place for the enemy to covertly control our lives. We must dislodge the lies that are obstacles to freedom. We begin by honestly admitting that all our thoughts, feelings, beliefs, attitudes which do not line up with the Bible are not Truth. In this process, denial is an enormous, but common, defense mechanism to protect us from pain, guilt and sin. If we do not want to deal with an issue, we simply pretend it is not there! We also need to recognize other coping mechanisms like flight, being late, fighting, and numbing out—and their role in how we deal with our shame.

Even our temperaments affect how we deal with our strongholds. According to one explanation of human behavior, there are four basic temperaments: phlegmatic, melancholy, sanguine and choleric. Each temperament has a different approach to dealing with shame. The phlegmatic will often put it off and never want to deal with it. The melancholy will look inside, evaluate and be very hard on himself. The sanguine will try to cover it up and move onto something more pleasant. The choleric will stuff it down and act like it's not there, so he can get on to another accomplishment. Knowing your temperament, as well as the temperaments of others around you, may be helpful in understanding how you deal with shame and other issues.

Shame-based people accustomed to wearing masks may even fear people with prophetic or revelatory giftings who try to help them. We don't want them to go behind the walls we have built to cover our shame. Fear of the prophetic is twofold—first, that they will know what is behind the walls and, second, that they will not deal with us lovingly and kindly.

Many issues may arise as we begin to recognize and identify our sources and patterns of shame. We usually find inner vows and judgments that need to be dealt with. A major thing to watch for is hard-heartedness due to vows and judgments. Another common part of the stronghold structure is soul-ties which bind us to the past. Demons have found a house of lies in our life; thus they are able to do their work often undetected. We must be determined to recognize and destroy these strongholds as we close the doors which have opened our life to the enemy. Freedom is our birthright!

> We built a shame-based life brick by brick. We often have to dismantle it brick by brick.

Another key is to totally embrace the healing process—and it is a process. Many do not want to go through it; they want a miracle of freedom. Sometimes, God does give us a miracle, and it's done and over with. However, that is not the norm. Generally, God requires us to go *through* the process. We built a shame-based life brick by brick. We often have to dismantle it brick by brick, because it is so connected with our distorted system of thoughts and beliefs. It's not just about tearing something down. The lies have to be replaced with Truth. That is the renewing of our mind by which we are transformed.

> And do not be conformed to this world, but be transformed by the renewing of your mind, that you may prove what is that good and acceptable and perfect will of God. (Romans 12:2)

We all can be instruments in helping to restore honor and dignity to others. Giving a person acceptance without judgment helps to communicate the true basis of his or her worth. People feel judgment in their spirit even if nothing is said in words. We receive others in the same way Christ has received us. Humility understands that God's grace alone makes us all acceptable.

Another important aspect of overcoming shame is to release true forgiveness to those who have hurt us. I am convinced that most people do not really know how to forgive, and that is why they don't do it. It is not that they don't want to. Forgiveness is a heart transaction and involves the emotions as well as the will.

> Humility understands that God's grace alone makes us all acceptable.

To pursue freedom, it is essential that we identify the lies that have bound us to shame. Then we repent of believing them and renounce them. We choose to embrace the truth instead of the lie. The next two chapters will help you identify many of the lies you have believed. The truth always sets you free if you embrace it.

And you shall know the truth, and the truth shall make you free. (John 8:32)

You cannot defend the lies that hold you and become free. You must embrace what God says about the lies. I was shamed much of my life because I believed the lie that "no one loves me". I thought people cared about me only because of what I could do for them. I was earning love with my work. Actually, I was loved. When I embraced the truth instead of my feelings, I was set free. It is our individual responsibility to pursue freedom from toxic shame. God does not want us to live like that. Jesus died to give us a new identity. Now let's take it back from the thief who kills, steals, and destroys!

CHAPTER EIGHTEEN

WRONG VIEWS OF GOD

he major obstacle to our walking in freedom from shame is simply our wrong belief system about who God is. We don't really know *Adonai Elohim* (Hebrew - LORD OF LORDS). We only know the "God" formed in our mind by all the lies we have believed. Until we can embrace the truth about who God really is, we will be in bondage to our faulty views of His person and character.

DOES GOD REALLY LOVE ME?

One foundational wrong view is we don't believe at our heart level that God truly loves us. We have interpreted who God is by our life's experience, not by Scripture. Long before we can read, understand and believe what the Bible says about God, we are exposed to various *messages*. A child rejected at birth by one or both parents is not yet able to understand in the soul - mind, will and emotions - that God is greater than his mother or father. Since God is a spirit and cannot be seen or touched, the child is limited to what he experiences in a given moment. Often, this locks us into a certain mindset. We can embrace the truth only to the degree that the lie is exposed. Much of the church today is not truly confident that God really loves them. They are locked into the experience of what they feel, and they have not yet *experienced* His love in a personal way. What difference does it make if God is all-powerful, if He is unwilling to use that power to help me? Unless I truly *know* and *feel* His love, I may believe He will meet everyone's needs except mine. I may even be able to pray effectively for others, because I'm sure He will help *them*!

WHO MAKES ALL THESE BAD THINGS HAPPEN?

Another wrong concept is that, since God is sovereign and controls all things, He makes bad things happen to me. I often hear people say that God took a child's mother in death because God needed her in heaven. "She was the most beautiful flower in the garden, so God picked her today because He wanted her." God is not a killer looking for someone to murder so other people will suffer. Certainly, God is in control, and bad things do happen. But evil and death have come because of sin. The devil has come to kill, steal and destroy (John 10:10). Death took the child's mother but, if she is a believer, Jesus took her from death and carried her to heaven. If we blame God for all the bad things in life, it shows that we have a wrong view of Him. God is the one who brings something good out of evil and wrong.

> We can embrace the truth only to the degree that the lie is exposed.

> And we know that all things work together for **good** to those who love God, to those who are the called according to His purpose. (Romans 8:28 – emphasis added)

WHY DON'T I HAVE WHAT I WANT?

Another view we must change is the belief that "God is withholding from me what I need." We want to blame Him for the lack in our life. Satan loves to set us up to accuse God. When we don't have enough money to pay the bills or anything we can define as lack, we want to fault God. Sometimes, it may even be caused by poor planning on our part. God has no desire to create lack in our life so we can suffer. For many years, I blamed God for my parents' divorce and for all the pain that came with it. I believed He should have prevented it. Out of His mercy, God took that which was evil and bad and brought good to my life. Job did not blame the Lord for the wind which came out of the wilderness and killed his seven sons. Although God often works in ways we don't understand, we must embrace the truth that He is good.

CAN I REALLY TRUST WHAT GOD SAYS?

Another judgment—God is not faithful. He doesn't fulfill His promises. This lie is embedded in early childhood so we won't trust Jesus as our Lord and Savior, and that casts doubt and unbelief in other areas. Consequently, I always had a Plan B in place, if Plan A did not work out. This mindset keeps you from trusting God to provide for you. With a few perceived failures in this department, I came to believe, "If you don't look out for yourself, no one else will." I was a hard worker; and God *let* me work hard because I did not believe in His desire to do good things for me. Never trusting God brings lots of shame into our life. It drives us to embrace the victim mentality, "It always happens to me." We believe Murphy's Law—If anything bad *can* happen, it *will*! Satan has a wonderful time punishing you and then telling you it was God who did it. The devil, not God, is the author of evil.

> The devil, not God, is the author of evil.

DOES GOD FORGIVE AND FORGET?

Another belief we need to let go is "God withholds things to punish me, because I have sinned." Becoming His child is about being forgiven. We humans have created classifications for sin and brand certain sins as worse than others. God forgives this sin but not that one. It required as much of Jesus' blood to forgive you for lying as it does for murder. God does not have a sliding scale on forgiveness. Either He has removed all your sins, or He hasn't. If He *has*, then believe with your whole heart that, **"It is finished."**

> As far as the east is from the west, so far has He removed our transgressions from us. (Psalm 103:12)

I received a letter from a young man asking for help. Bill poured out his heart about trying to get churches, pastors and other ministers to help him and no one would or could. He thought I was his last cry for help. He was rejected at birth because his father wanted a girl. He was raised in an extreme fundamental religious home under a lot of condemnation. He never measured up at home or in church. He was molested by a pastor in his early teens. He then went into a homosexual lifestyle. Later he became a drag queen. From there, his life went even further into degradation. He said, "I am not saved and I have sinned too much for God to save me. God would not want someone like me." Two of my team members met with him, led him to Jesus and set him free from the strongholds and lies that bound him to sin. Today, he is still serving the Lord. The Apostle Paul said he was the chief of sinners and God saved him so your sins are forgivable. There's no such thing as a sin so bad that God cannot and will not forgive. Jesus paid for every one of your sins on the cross so you could receive forgiveness for all your sins.

> *Becoming His child is about being forgiven.*

This is a faithful saying and worthy of all acceptance, that Christ Jesus came into the world to save sinners, of whom I am chief. (1 Timothy 1:15)

WHERE IS GOD ANYWAY?

Another wrong view of God is that He is hiding Himself and His will from me. Many have the view of God, that He is so holy and so high up in heaven that I could never know him. Or that God is a reluctant God who hides from us and does not want to be known. The truth is God wants you to know him and He wants to know you. God is not silent in heaven playing some kind of game of hide and seek. God desires to know you and wants you to know Him. The very purpose of his son's death and resurrection was that He could have a relationship with you.

My sheep hear My voice, and I know them, and they follow Me. (John 10:27)

From that statement we know that God wants to talk to us and wants us to fellowship with Him. We must embrace the truth that God desires to know us and be known by us.

How Good Do I Have to Be?

A perspective we must break free from is the opinion that God will let us go to heaven because we are good. Nowhere in scripture does it say that you can earn your way into the presence of God. We have no ability to set ourselves right with God apart from the blood of Jesus Christ. It is not by works of righteousness that God accepts us but by the blood of Jesus, His substitutionary blood for all of our sinfulness. We are brought to God by the grace of Jesus.

> For by grace you have been saved through faith, and that not of yourselves; it is the gift of God, not of works, lest anyone should boast. For we are His workmanship, created in Christ Jesus for good works, which God prepared beforehand that we should walk in them. (Ephesians 2:8-10)

The only way to God is through the blood of Jesus Christ.

> But to him who does not work but believes on Him who justifies the ungodly, his faith is accounted for righteousness. (Romans 4:5)

Eternal life comes by Jesus' death at the cross. When I have repented of my sins, believed in my heart and received Him into my life, I am righteous. It is a gift.

You Owe Me!

Another misconception is that God has promised a totally happy, trouble-free, easy, healthy life to His children. We equate what God calls an abundant life with a life free of problems. Often we lift out of scripture conditional promises and *claim* the promise with no regard to meeting the condition of obedience. Then we are mad at God because He has let us down. We may even accept the lie that God has reserved good for a special few. God does not have favorites in His kingdom. His principles apply to everyone. It may be that we do not understand the laws of sowing and reaping. If we sow we shall reap. If we give it shall be given to us. If we love others, love comes back to us. Somehow we experience, early in life, the opposites of God's kingdom. So we don't believe on a heart level that God's promises are true. Let's take the law of sowing and reaping. Many sow only a few seeds but expect a great harvest.

> The true God does not heap shame on His creation. He sent His Son to remove it!

They are totally confused and discouraged when what they expected did not happen. Any farmer will tell you that if you want a bountiful crop, you must also plant bountiful seed. Only what you plant will come up. You must plant and keep on planting. You cannot plant once and reap for a lifetime. Many plant one time and they blame God for not having an abundant life. We must develop a life of sowing, all the time, in every place we can if we want abundance. You cannot blame God for a small harvest if you only sow in a small manner. The problem is not God but our wrong view of God.

We could go on and on about the faulty perceptions of God. We must repent of our unbelief, turn to God and seek to know Him as He really is. We must begin to meditate on God's revelation of Himself in the scriptures. God knew we would have a difficult time understanding an invisible God. So Jesus Christ was made flesh so we could see God in human form. If you want to know the heart of God, read the gospels again and take a fresh look at Jesus. He told the disciples, "If you have seen me, you have seen the Father." As we correct our view of God, our lives will turn from lack to plenty, from shame to honor, from failure to success. We must know God as He truly is and not as we have imagined – an image created in our own mind. The true God does not heap shame on His creation. He sent His Son to remove it!

CHAPTER NINETEEN

IDENTIFYING THE LIES I HAVE BELIEVED

"If you continue in my Word, then are you my disciples indeed, and you shall know the truth, and the truth shall make you free." (John 8:31-32)

If this is the Lord's reality, why do we continue in our shame? We have believed that knowing the truth means we have mental understanding of it; therefore, we should walk in freedom. Jesus was not talking about intellectual comprehension, but rather about an *experiential* knowing of the truth. The word "know" means to be intimate with in order to reproduce.

Now Adam knew Eve his wife and she conceived. (Genesis 4:1)

Here, the word "know" means "to be intimate with in order to reproduce." If you want to really know the truth, you must take it home with you and sleep with it. The American church puts much emphasis on knowing things in our minds, but that will not change us. If we *know* them in our spirit and in our heart, only then will we be changed. The great lie—I *know* the truth—keeps us locked in bondage. It really comes down to the question, "Do I believe the Word of God or not?"

Another life-encompassing lie is God has kept back something I need.

And my God shall supply all your need according to His riches in glory by Christ Jesus. (Philippians 4:19)

Somehow, He created a need and has not met it. Therefore, I must get it myself.

It may even be a legitimate need, but I will try to fulfill it in an illegitimate way. This is the lie Adam and Eve believed in the Garden of Eden. Satan was successful in placing in Eve a sense of lack to get her to eat the fruit. If Adam and Eve had believed in their identity, they would not have accepted the lie. In their minds, the feeling of lack justified the decision to disobey God. We are tempted the same way today. When we believe the lie about our lack, we have the audacity, in independence and rebellion, to try to meet our own needs. Adam gave up his wholeness because "God did not give me His best". He did not believe he was already created in God's image and so set out to establish his own identity. Thus, shame and fear came immediately into his life. To the degree we are motivated by fear is the degree we have accepted the mindset of lack.

When Satan came to Jesus in the temptation (Matthew 4), he used the same strategy that he had used on Adam, appealing to the lack. Satan tried to get Jesus to prove His identity by performing miracles. If Jesus had taken that challenge, it would show He didn't believe Who He truly is. Since Jesus did not acknowledge any lack in His life, the enemy's trick failed. Jesus was totally connected to the sense of fullness in the Father. When your identity in Jesus becomes your reality, circumstances will no longer be able to control you. We live out of who we are, not out of what we can do. To break out of the fear and shame that control us, we must release the assumptions we have about ourselves. To destroy you, Satan does not need you to deny Jesus as your Lord and Savior, but only to believe that what Jesus did and gave was not enough.

> To the degree we are motivated by fear is the degree we have accepted the mindset of lack.

Another deception Satan uses against us also concerns our identity. Jesus is the Son of God who died to give us back all that we lost in Adam's sin. If we don't believe it, we are choosing to reject the truth.

> Therefore, if anyone is in Christ, he is a new creation; old things have passed away; behold, all things have become new. (2 Corinthians 5:17)

I have been restored to God's original intent. I am given a new identity. The problem often is that we don't believe it. God's word seems too good to be true.

> For in Him dwells all the fullness of the Godhead bodily; and you are complete in Him, who is the head of all principality and power. (Colossians 2:9-10)

Therefore, if I am complete in Him, I lack nothing. Jesus has given me *His* completeness. I need only to believe that I am *totally* restored. If I truly do believe it, I will automatically begin to live it out.

In the womb or in early childhood, if a person is not wanted, loved, accepted and owned, the assumption is made that he or she is a mistake. Children do not have the capacity to sort out lies from truth. They believe what is communicated to their spirits. Shame covers such children like a shroud. They are confused about who their real father is – Father God.

If I truly believe it, I will automatically begin to live it out.

> Then God said, "Let Us make man in Our image, according to Our likeness; let them have dominion over the fish of the sea, over the birds of the air, and over the cattle, over all the earth and over every creeping thing that creeps on the earth." (Genesis 1:26)

Yes, we have a man we call our earthly father, but he and our earthly mother did not create us. God, our heavenly Father, created us. (Psalm 139:13-16) Our real Father has never rejected, disowned, abandoned, or hated us. He has always loved and received us. Once we can see we are a child of the Most High God, the lie melts away. We no longer need to wear a mask. We may never receive our earthly parent's approval, but we are able to live life to the fullest if we know we have our Heavenly Father's love. We are on our way to becoming who we really are!

I ministered to a 50-year-old woman who came to me because she could not function in her church or her family without crying and losing control of her emotions. On the day of her birth, her father cursed her because she was a female. He had so wanted a son that he was already referring to her as a boy while she was still in the womb. He rejected her and never owned her as his child. When her brother was born two years later, the father basically abandoned her.

His job took him out of the home Monday through Friday. Weekends were used for *his* needs, *his* business and catering to the younger brother. This little girl was so desperate for love that, in the first grade, she kissed all the boys in the class. One day, she bragged that she had kissed Johnny *six times*! She became sexually active in her teen-age years and became pregnant in her senior year. Her mother arranged for an abortion. She went to college and slept around with numerous men, looking for someone to love her. But all she got was sex, not love. Then, she had a radical conversion and joined a campus ministry. But, being trained for full-time ministry and loving God did not fill the deep hole in her heart. She occasionally fell into sin. Each time, with deep repentance, she announced to God that she would never fall again and promised Him faithfulness. She later married a man in ministry, but she could never stop crying and losing control of her emotions. She and her husband were serving very faithfully in a large church, but the senior pastor and his wife could not find out what was the problem. That day in my office, God became real to her, and she experienced the love of her Father in heaven. God healed her broken heart, cleansed her from all her failures, gave her a true identity and took away her shame. She now knows experientially that she is a daughter of the King, and she serves the Lord with joy and pleasure. Her heart is healed because she has accepted who she *really* is in Jesus Christ.

> Our real Father has never rejected, disowned, abandoned, or hated us. He has always loved and received us.

Another lie we have believed is, "If God loved me, I would be happy." God never promised us a life of roses and pleasant experiences; He promised to provide and care for us. Actually, He has promised us difficulty and struggles, because God wants to work joy in our life. Joy, not happiness, is the fruit of the spirit in Galatians 5:22. Shame keeps us from experiencing moments of happiness in life, because shame says, "God does not love me. Things happen (or don't happen) because God does not love me." We can either believe or reject what Scripture says about God's feelings for us.

"Greater love has no one than this, than to lay down one's life for his friends." (John 15:13)

"For God so loved the world that He gave His only begotten Son, that whoever believes in Him should not perish but have everlasting life." (John 3:16)

By this we know love, because He laid down His life for us. And we also ought to lay down our lives for the brethren. (1 John 3:16)

"I drew them with gentle cords, with bands of love." (Hosea 11:4)

"Yes, I have loved you with an everlasting love; Therefore with lovingkindness I have drawn you." (Jeremiah 31:3)

And we have known and believed the love that God has for us. **God is love**, and he who abides in love abides in God, and God in him (emphasis added). (1 John 4:16)

But God, who is rich in mercy, because of His great love with which He loved us, even when we were dead in trespasses, made us alive together with Christ. (Ephesians 2:4-5)

The last lie we will investigate is the lie that God is not just. "God has really dealt me a bum hand. I've had all kinds of difficulties and heartaches, because He is not a just God. If He were, I would not be where I am!" How many of you understand you *have to* play the hand God deals you? For many years, I was very angry with God because my parents had divorced. In my mid-thirties, I was pastoring a church in Irving, Texas, and I said to Him one day, "What kind of God are you anyway? You're not able, not powerful, not loving at all. You couldn't even keep my mom and dad together, so I had to be the only child in my first grade class from a broken home. I have suffered all kinds of deep rejection, because you're not a just God!" In a very gentle, loving voice, He spoke to me, "Henry, your problem is you don't see life the way I see it. You're looking through a knothole in the fence at a parade going by. You see a line of trombone players and think they are the whole parade. You think that all music comes from just one instrument, the trombone. You don't see all the other instruments, floats and entries. Your view of the parade is distorted, just like your view of life is

> God knows the end from the beginning and has given you everything that you need to succeed in life.

distorted. I allowed these things to happen in order to prepare you for what I have called you to—your destiny."

Today I am who I am because of our just God. He dealt me the hand I needed to become *myself*. I experienced deep rejection, and that prepared me to help thousands of others in similar situations. Don't rage at God because of your tears, your pain, and your difficulties. He knows the end from the beginning and has given you everything that you need to succeed in life.

I ministered to Kenneth, a young man whose family had broken up, and he suffered deep rejection and abandonment by his parents. But I could never get him to give up his view that God was unjust. He was very angry and refused to let go of the hurts of his life, choosing to keep his shame and live in defeat. He blamed everyone else for his misfortunes, especially his mother and father. He acknowledged God with his lips, but his heart was far from Him. He turned his back on God's grace.

God wants to free us from shame. We must choose. We can hold onto the lies Satan has told us and what our experiences have convinced us are true. If we continue down that path, we will reject the *real* truth and never find God's best for our lives. Jesus is the Truth. He said, "I am truth; I am the way to God." When we embrace Him, the lies will melt away from us. And with the lies -- the shame.

CHAPTER TWENTY

SHAME-FREE:
FINDING MY TRUE IDENTITY

As a man thinks in his heart, so is he. (Proverbs 23:7)

You are who you think you are. Why? Because you live out what you
believe about yourself. We all remember the story of the man who starved
to death because he thought he had no money. Yet after he died, it was
discovered he had over a million dollars in the bank. An uncle had left him
the money in his will. But, because the man believed he had nothing, he died
of starvation and neglect. We're not much different, if we do not know who
we really are in Christ. We will never live like the King's kids. We will always
be living the lie rather than the truth.

John 21:1-19 tells the story of Peter who returned to fishing after
denying Jesus three times, once even with anger and cursing. Peter could
not stand it anymore. He believed the God of Heaven had turned His back
on him. Peter put it this way, "I'm returning to what I am—a fisherman; I'm
going fishing." He knew he had let Jesus down, so he believed he was a failure.
Now he was even failing at fishing. He caught nothing all night long. The
next morning, when Jesus told Peter to cast the net on the other side, it came
back full. Peter knew it was the Lord who had done that. He jumped in the
water and swam to shore, and Jesus offered him fellowship and acceptance.
Jesus' question, "Do you love me?" was a hard one for Peter. When he said,

"Yes, I love You", He gave him the assignment of feeding and loving the sheep. Peter received a *new identity*. Three times the Lord asked that question, and three times Peter responded with the same answer. Each time, Jesus gave him the assignment of feeding and caring for others.

We must have a new identity. We're all born in the same condition— separated from God. Each of us must come to the place of personally accepting Jesus Christ as our Lord and Savior. Thus we become new creations, and the Holy Spirit conforms us to the image of the Son. That's our new identity—in Him!

> That if you confess with your mouth the Lord Jesus and believe in your heart that God has raised Him from the dead, you will be saved. For with the heart one believes unto righteousness, and with the mouth confession is made unto salvation. (Romans 10:9-10)

Believing in the heart is so much more than just gathering intellectual information. Many people believe that God raised Jesus from the dead, but that has not changed their lives. There are two schools of thought here. One is from the Greek, and the other from the Hebrew. To *know* to the Greek means to "have acquired the information you need and filed it in your brain". To the Jew, you do not *know* something until you have believed it; believing it has changed your life and become a part of who you are. For example, would you like to fly in an airplane with a pilot who has only read books about flying and watched a few planes take off and land at the airport? I would not trust my life to a person like that. That is the Greek way of knowing. I want a pilot who has read the books, watched the planes take off and land *and* has practiced—until flying has changed his life.

> We're all born in the same condition— separated from God.

You may remember the story of Jessica Dubroff as she took off from Cheyenne, Wyoming, on the morning of April 11, 1996. Jessica was a seven-year-old who wanted to win the record for being the youngest person ever to successfully complete a continental flight. She loved flying and was all excited about her coming victory. In an attempt to beat a storm front, she and her father and a flight instructor took off with rain and sleet coming down. The plane stalled within a few minutes, and all on board were killed. She did not have the breadth of experience to go with her little bit of knowledge, and it led to her premature death.

Knowing about God is not the same as knowing God. To *know* Him, I have to experience Him in my heart, and my life will be changed as a result. You can be born again and not really know who you are in Christ. This knowledge can be limited because of all the lies you have believed about who God really is. I allowed the lie that "No one really loves me" to keep me from *knowing* His love. The enemy also provided numerous circumstances which I accepted as rejection. All this kept me bound in shame. When I experienced God's true love for me,

> Knowing about God is not the same as knowing God.

those lies melted like butter in the hot sun. The only thing that will take away your shame is for you to *experience* in your heart, His wonderful love for you. All the books and scriptures about how much He loves you will not necessarily change anything. Head knowledge must become heart knowledge to bring change in your life. In order to live in my true identity, I must know God loves me and believe His plan for my life is good.

The enemy's lie that God is not good keeps us looking for all the wrong things in life, which *proves* He is bad. God desires only what is best for us now and in the life to come. Often Satan will steal from us and tell us God is withholding it from us. "See there? God is not good. You asked Him for this, and He said, 'No.' He will always hold out on you when you want or need something." Because God is omniscient, He knows what is best for each of us. When a child asks for ice cream just before dinner and the parent says, "No," the parent is really being good to the child. But the child is angry, because he did not get what he wanted when he wanted it. Realizing that God loves me unconditionally and desires what is best for me provides a foundation of trust that will hold firm through the temptations, trials and struggles I face in life.

Another important shift into my new identity is the understanding that Christ's righteousness is given to me as a free gift.

> For He made Him who knew no sin to be sin for us, that we might become the righteousness of God in Him. (2 Corinthians 5:21)

Jesus took our sin and in exchange, He gave us His righteousness. Righteousness is an absolute. You cannot be partially righteous—you either have all of Jesus' righteousness or you have none.

> But we are all like an unclean thing, and all our righteousnesses are like filthy rags. (Isaiah 64:6)

If we **know** we are righteous, righteous attitudes and actions will begin to flow from us.

Since we are unable to produce it within ourselves, our only hope is to accept the righteousness of Jesus. Remember, we live out who we believe we are. If we know we are righteous, righteous attitudes and actions will begin to flow from us. Some of our confusion on this subject may concern holiness. My holiness is a work in progress, but my righteousness is an absolute.

> It is written, "Be holy, for I am holy." (1 Peter 1:16)

My New Identity

As I believe that I am accepted, loved and righteous, I begin to live out my true identity in Christ. If you are struggling to accept the reality of your new identity, it would greatly benefit you to practice the following exercises: For the next 40 days . . .

- Read these scriptures.
- Meditate on them.
- Personalize them.
- Visualize the truth about yourself.
- Believe them in your heart.
- Refuse the self-talk that says anything different.
- Break the negative patterns of thinking.
- Bring your thoughts and words into line with the word of God. As you do this, your heart's belief system will shift.

1. I AM A CHILD OF GOD.

But as many as received Him, to them He gave the right to become children of God, to those who believe in His name. (John 1:12)

For you are all sons of God through faith in Christ Jesus. (Galatians 3:26)

2. I AM THE RIGHTEOUSNESS OF CHRIST.

For He made Him who knew no sin to be sin for us, that we might become the righteousness of God in Him. (2 Corinthians 5:21)

And having been set free from sin, you became slaves of righteousness. (Romans 6:18)

3. I AM A NEW CREATION.

Therefore, if anyone is in Christ, he is a new creation; old things have passed away; behold, all things have become new. (2 Corinthians 5:17)

What shall we say then? Shall we continue in sin that grace may abound? Certainly not! How shall we who died to sin live any longer in it? Or do you not know that as many of us as were baptized into Christ Jesus were baptized into His death? Therefore we were buried with Him through baptism into death, that just as Christ was raised from the dead by the glory of the Father, even so we also should walk in newness of life.

For if we have been united together in the likeness of His death, certainly we also shall be in the likeness of His resurrection, knowing this, that our old man was crucified with Him, that the body of sin might be done away with, that we should no longer be slaves of sin. For he who has died has been freed from sin. Now if we died with Christ, we believe that we shall also live with Him, knowing that Christ, having been raised from the dead, dies no more. Death no longer has dominion over Him. For the death that He died, He died to sin once for all; but the life that He lives, He lives to God. Likewise you also, reckon yourselves to be dead indeed to sin, but alive to God in Christ Jesus our Lord. (Romans 6:1-11)

4. I AM THE DWELLING PLACE OF GOD: A TEMPLE OF CHRIST.

Do you not know that you are the temple of God and that the Spirit of God dwells in you? (1 Corinthians 3:16)

Or do you not know that your body is the temple of the Holy Spirit who is in you, whom you have from God, and you are not your own? (1 Corinthians 6:19)

But he who is joined to the Lord is one spirit with Him. (1 Corinthians 6:17)

5. I AM A PART OF THE TRUE VINE, AND I AM APPOINTED TO BEAR FRUIT.

"I am the true vine, and My Father is the vinedresser. Every branch in Me that does not bear fruit He takes away; and every branch that bears fruit He prunes, that it may bear more fruit." (John 15:1-2)

"I am the vine, you are the branches. He who abides in Me, and I in him, bears much fruit; for without Me you can do nothing." (John 15:5)

"You did not choose Me, but I chose you and appointed you that you should go and bear fruit, and that your fruit should remain, that whatever you ask the Father in My name He may give you." (John 15:16)

6. I AM A PART OF THE BODY OF CHRIST.

Now you are the body of Christ, and members individually. (1 Corinthians 12:27)

For we are members of His body, of His flesh and of His bones. (Ephesians 5:30)

7. I AM AN HEIR OF GOD.

And if children, then heirs — heirs of God and joint heirs with Christ, if indeed we suffer with Him, that we may also be glorified together. (Romans 8:17)

Therefore you are no longer a slave but a son, and if a son, then an heir of God through Christ. (Galatians 4:7)

8. I AM A SAINT.

To the church of God which is at Corinth, to those who are sanctified in Christ Jesus, called to be saints, with all who in every place call on the name of Jesus Christ our Lord, both theirs and ours. (1 Corinthians 1:2)

To all who are in Rome, beloved of God, called to be saints. (Romans 1:7)

9. I AM RIGHTEOUS AND HOLY.

And that you put on the new man, which was created according to God, in true righteousness and holiness. (Ephesians 4:24)

But now we have been delivered from the law, having died to what we were held by, so that we should serve in the newness of the Spirit and not in the oldness of the letter. (Romans 7:6)

10. I AM HIS WORKMANSHIP.

For we are His workmanship, created in Christ Jesus for good works, which God prepared beforehand that we should walk in them. (Ephesians 2:10)

11. I AM A CITIZEN OF HEAVEN.

And raised us up together, and made us sit together in the heavenly places in Christ Jesus. (Ephesians 2:6)

Now, therefore, you are no longer strangers and foreigners, but fellow citizens with the saints and members of the household of God. (Ephesians 2:19)

12. I AM AN EXPRESSION OF THE LIFE OF CHRIST.

For you died, and your life is hidden with Christ in God. When Christ who is our life appears, then you also will appear with Him in glory. (Colossians 3:3-4)

To them God willed to make known what are the riches of the glory of this mystery among the Gentiles: which is Christ in you, the hope of glory. (Colossians 1:27)

For we have become partakers of Christ if we hold the beginning of our confidence steadfast to the end. (Hebrews 3:14)

13. I AM A ROYAL PRIEST.

But you are a chosen generation, a royal priesthood, a holy nation, His own special people, that you may proclaim the praises of Him who called you out of darkness into His marvelous light; who once were not a people but are now the people of God, who had not obtained mercy but now have obtained mercy. (1 Peter 2:9-10)

14. I AM A LIVING STONE MADE INTO A HOME FOR GOD.

You also, as living stones, are being built up a spiritual house, a holy priesthood, to offer up spiritual sacrifices acceptable to God through Jesus Christ. (1 Peter 2:5)

15. I AM AN ALIEN TO THIS WORLD.

Likewise you also, reckon yourselves to be dead indeed to sin, but alive to God in Christ Jesus our Lord. (Romans 6:11)

For sin shall not have dominion over you, for you are not under law but under grace. (Romans 6:14)

Behold what manner of love the Father has bestowed on us, that we should be called children of God! Therefore the world does not know us, because it did not know Him. Beloved, now we are children of

God; and it has not yet been revealed what we shall be, but we know that when He is revealed, we shall be like Him, for we shall see Him as He is. (1 John 3:1-2)

16. I am more than a conqueror in Christ.

We know that whoever is born of God does not sin; but he who has been born of God keeps himself, and the wicked one does not touch him. (1 John 5:1)

Yet in all these things we are more than conquerors through Him who loved us. (Romans 8:37)

17. I am complete in Christ.

For in Him dwells all the fullness of the Godhead bodily; and you are complete in Him, who is the head of all principality and power. (Colossians 2:9-10)

For we have become partakers of Christ if we hold the beginning of our confidence steadfast to the end. (Hebrews 3:14)

18. I am the enemy of the devil.

Be sober, be vigilant; because your adversary the devil walks about like a roaring lion, seeking whom he may devour. (1 Peter 5:8)

Therefore submit to God. Resist the devil and he will flee from you. (James 4:7)

You can be free from the toxic shame that steals your identity. If you are God's child, you have a new identity in Christ. Jesus refused to receive toxic shame that came to Him; he did not identify with it as His own. Instead, on the cross, He took our shame upon Himself so that we could walk and live shame-free.

"I gave My back to those who struck Me,
And My cheeks to those who plucked out the beard;

I did not hide My face from shame and spitting.
For the Lord GOD will help Me;
Therefore I will not be disgraced;
Therefore I have set My face like a flint,
And I know that I will not be ashamed." (Isaiah 50:6-7)

Jesus did not run from shame; He faced it head-on. Sometimes, you may want to run, but don't give in to those desires. You must put your trust in God. Jesus had confidence that God would remove the shame from Him. Our shame is gone by the power of the resurrection. When Jesus was resurrected, He left His shame and ours in the grave. When Jesus rose from the dead, we rose with Him. Our pathway to glory is in the receiving of the life of Christ within us. Set your affections on Jesus and believe.

And whoever believes on Him will not be put to shame. (Romans 9:33)

If I will trust Him, God will give me the answer to those who try to shame me.

Let Your mercies come also to me, O LORD –
Your salvation according to Your word.
So shall I have an answer for him who reproaches me,
For I trust in Your word. (Psalm 119:41-42)

I must hide truth in my heart and trust God to lead my life. Truth has a powerfully transforming effect in our lives. Truth will keep us looking up to God.

All Scripture is given by inspiration of God, and is profitable for doctrine, for reproof, for correction, for instruction in righteousness, that the man of God may be complete, thoroughly equipped for every good work. (2 Timothy 3:16-17)

If you do not know that you are a child of God, you have no avenue to find freedom from shame. But today, you can change that. Simply repent before God for your rebellion, and ask Jesus to forgive you of all your sins. You might pray something like this:

"Heavenly Father, I confess to You that I have sinned. My sins are wicked and ungodly. I repent of trying to run my life without You. Please forgive me of my sins. Come into my life, and make me a new person. I receive all that Jesus did for me on the cross and accept Him as my Lord and Savior. Thank you, Father, for saving me and forgiving my sins. Amen."

If you are already a child of God, but have allowed shame to maintain a heavy grip on your life and steal your identity, you can pray something like this:

"Dear Heavenly Father, please send your Spirit to heal me. Take me back to a memory of shame that damaged me. At that very moment, Satan planted a lie in my spirit. Reveal that lie to me, and let me see it clearly. (Wait as the Holy Spirit reveals a past experience that imprinted shame upon you.) Separate the lie from my memory so I can be free. In that memory, there was someone who hurt me, and I've never been healed. Father, I choose to forgive that person. I let go of my need for revenge. Father, I also repent of hating myself and believing the lie I was told. Please come and shatter that lie. I choose to take off the mask I've worn, and I come to you just as I am. Holy Spirit, show me the truth of who I am in Christ. (Wait as the Holy Spirit shows you the truth.) Thank You, Lord. I receive the truth. I receive my new identity. In Jesus' name. Amen."

If you follow these suggestions but find yourself still locked into shame, you need to seek out someone to minister to you. Find a person who understands inner healing and deliverance. Ask them to use their authority to break the power of the enemy that is holding you in bondage to shame. Jesus died to set you free.

For this purpose the Son of God was manifested, that He might destroy the works of the devil. (1 John 3:8b)

To Him be all honor and glory and power forever!

ENDNOTES

CHAPTER 1

1   *Experiencing the Father's Embrace,* Jack Frost (Charisma House, Lake Mary, FL, 2002)
2   *Shame, Our Hidden Torment,* Grant Mullen, (2-CD Series, Burlington, Ontario, Canada, Orchardview Medical Media, 2004)
3   *Healing the Shame That Binds You,* John Bradshaw, (Health Communications, Inc., Deerfield Beach, FL,1988)
4   *Living From the Heart Jesus Gave You,* James G. Friesen, E. James Wilder, Anne M. Bierling, Rick Koepcke and Maribeth Poole, Kearney, NE, Morris Publishing, 1999)

CHAPTER 2

5   Healing the Shame that Binds You, John Bradshaw (Health Communications, Inc., Deerfield Beach, FL, 1988)
6   Shame Video, Part 1, Sandra Sellmer (Elijah House Ministries, Spokane, WA)
7   IBID

CHAPTER 3

8   *Healing the Shame That Binds You,* John Bradshaw, (Deerfield Beach, FL, Health Communications, Inc., 1988)
9   IBID, Pg. 22
10 *Shame Tape Series,* Joe Medina (Daily Bread Ministries, Birmingham, AL)
11 *Shame Video, Part 1,* Sandra Sellmer (Elijah House Ministries, Spokane, WA)
12 *Living From the Heart Jesus Gave You,* James G. Friesen, James Wilder, Anne M. Bierling, Rick Koepcke and Maribeth Poole, (Shepherd's House, Inc., Pasadena, CA, 1999)

CHAPTER 4

13   *Shame Video, Part 1*, Sandra Sellmer (Elijah House Ministries, Spokane, WA)
14   IBID
15   *Shame Tape Series*, Joe Medina (Daily Bread Ministries, Birmingham, AL)

CHAPTER 5

16   *Shame and Grace*, Lewis B. Smedes, (Harper Collins Publishers, New York, NY, 1993)
17   *The Road Less Traveled*, Scott Peck, (Touchstone, New York, NY, 1978)
18   *Healing the Shame that Binds You*, John Bradshaw (Health Communications, Deerfield Beach, FL, 1988) Pg.8
19   *Healing the Shame that Binds You*, John Bradshaw (Health Communications, Inc., Deerfield Beach, FL, 1988), Pg. 8
20   IBID, Pg. 11
21   *For Your Own Good*, Alice Miller, (Noonday Press, 1990) Pg. 20
22   IBID

CHAPTER 6

23   *Shame, Our Hidden Torment*, 2-CD, Grant Mullen, (Orchardview Medical Media, Burlington, Ontario, Canada, 2004)
24   *Shame Free*, Bill and Sue Banks, (Impact Christian Books, Inc., Kirkwood, MO, 2002)
25   *Shame Off You*, Alan D. Wright, (Multnomah Publishers, Inc., Sisters, OR, 2005)

CHAPTER 7

26   *Shame Free*, Bill and Sue Banks, (Impact Christian Books, Inc., Kirkwood, MO, 2002)
27   *Facing Co-Dependency*, Pia Melody, (Harper Collins Publishers, Inc., New York, NY, 1989)
28   IBID
29   *Shame Tape Series*, Joe Medina (Daily Bread Ministries, Birmingham, AL)
30   IBID

CHAPTER 8

31   *Facing Co-Dependency*, Pia Melody, (Harper Collins, San Francisco, CA, 1989)
32   *Finding Freedom from the Shame of the Past*, Mike Fehlauer, (Charisma House, Lake Mary, FL, 1999)
33   IBID
34   *Shame Tape Series*, Joe Medina (Daily Bread Ministries, Birmingham, AL)
35   *Shame Video Series*, Sandra Sellmer (Elijah House Ministries, Spokane, WA)

CHAPTER 9

36   *Shame*, John Bradshaw (Health Communications, Inc., Deerfield, FL, 1988)
37   IBID

38 IBID, Pg. 39-40
39 *Shame Free*, Bill and Sue Banks, (Impact Christian Books, Inc., Kirkwood, MO, 2002)

Chapter 12

40 *Breaking the Cycle*, James Richards, (Impact Ministries, Huntsville, AL, 2003)

Chapter 13

41 *Healing the Wounded Heart*, Thom Gardner, (Destiny Image Publishers, Inc., Shippenburg, PA, 2005)

Chapter 14

42 *Breaking the Cycle*, James Richards, (Impact Ministries, Huntsville, AL, 2003)

Chapter 16

43 *Shame and Grace*, Lewis Smedes, (Harper Collins Publishers, New York, NY, 1993) Pg. 108
44 *Altars of the Heart*, Thom Gardner, (Destiny Image, Inc., Shippensburg, PA 2003)
45 *Shame and Grace*, Smedes, pg. 110-113
46 *Healing the Wounded Heart*, Thom Gardner, (Destiny Image, Inc., Shippensburg, PA, 2005)

Chapter 17

47 *Shame Tape Series*, Joe Medina (Daily Bread Ministries, Birmingham, AL)
48 *Healing the Shame that Binds You*, John Bradshaw, (Health Communications, Inc., Deerfield Beach, FL, 1988)
49 *Shame Tape Series*, Joe Medina (Daily Bread Ministries, Birmingham, AL)

ABOUT THE AUTHOR

Dr. Henry Malone is president and founder of Vision Life Ministries, a restoration and equipping ministry, designed to heal the brokenhearted, set at liberty those who are bruised and free those who are captive. Previously a senior pastor for 28 years, he has been ministering translocally to edify and build up the Body of Christ since 1989. Henry emphasizes demonstrating the works of the Kingdom as well as proclaiming the Gospel of the Kingdom. In 1994, he began the Freedom and Fullness Seminars which release the ministry of Jesus in a group setting to bring healing, deliverance and freedom.

Since 1992 he has trained and released interns for deliverance and emotional healing. In 1998 he began the Schools of Deliverance Ministry to expedite this training. This equipping has expanded into what is now the Personal Development Institute. His desire is to help local churches establish effective balanced deliverance ministries to fulfill the mandate of Luke 4:18. His training emphasizes the importance of Christ-like character and a servant's heart as well as the skill and anointing necessary to be vessels of honor in God's kingdom. Affiliated ministries and associate ministers who have been trained through VLM are helping to fulfill this vision throughout the nation. Henry's heart throbs with compassion for the bruised, the broken and the captive—a spirit which he imparts to those whom he "fathers."

He has written several books including Shadow Boxing, Portals to Cleansing, Islam Unmasked, and God's Miracle Land: Pakistan. Each year, Henry also helps train national pastors in several third-world pastors conferences as well as traveling to churches and conferences speaking on behalf of world missions.

He and his wife Tina have two grown children and four grandchildren and live in the Dallas, Texas area.

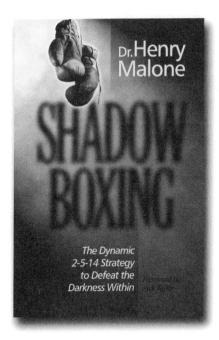

DEFEAT THE DARKNESS WITHIN

A powerful book by Dr. Malone

Discover the dynamic 2-5-14 strategy that will help you defeat the darkness within. Here is what people are saying about this life-changing book:

A fresh, unique, biblical and practical view on how to close doors to Satan. This book will lead many to liberty and fullness of life. **—James Robison**

This book will benefit and strengthen those who are living victory in spiritual life and unlock those who are being held in darkness! **—Chuck Pierce**

Also Available in Spanish! ▶

Get Your Copy Today!
Paperback—$13

Vision Life Publications
PO Box 153691 ♦ Irving, Texas 75015 ♦ www.visionlife.org

Take Back Spiritual Ground

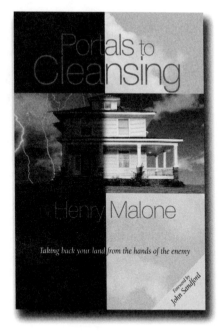

by
Dr. Malone

Portals—they exist all around the earth and open a door to the presence of God or to the demonic. Step into the realm of the supernatural with *Portals to Cleansing*. Discover how spiritual ground is taken and how it is released. Learn the keys to reclaiming your land, home, possessions and animals from the power of Satan and his demonic forces. Experience the peace that comes from the cleansing of all you possess. Walk into a portal of God's presence that will take you deeper into the realm of the Spirit and change your life forever.

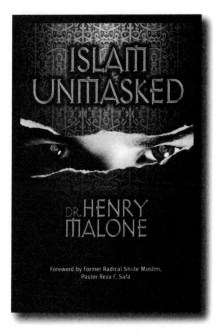

THE TRUTH ABOUT ISLAM

Also available by Dr. Malone

In a time of much media disinformation, filtered through unholy agendas, this book is a welcome relief. While God loves those of the Islam faith, He does not love the Islam faith itself. In **Islam Unmasked**, Henry Malone reveals the clear and present danger that Islam presents not only to the Body of Christ, but also to the world. Wise men will heed the warning contained herein.

—John Paul Jackson, Streams Ministries International

Following the horror of the September 11, 2001 attacks, many have been confused and deceived about Islam. *Islam Unmasked* uncovers the power and authority believers have over the deceptions of false religions. It delves into the history, origins, doctrines and deception behind Islam and reveals the truth about this fast-growing world religion. It also provides much needed insight into how believers can find the common ground for discussion with those who practice Islam and how they can break down the barriers to salvation through love.

Vision Life Publications
PO Box 153691 ◆ Irving, Texas 75015 ◆ www.visionlife.org

FREEDOM AND FULLNESS SEMINAR

Break free from spiritual bondage
and be released into the fullness of the Holy Spirit!

The cry of the human heart is for freedom, healing, wholeness and a lifestyle of peace, joy and fulfillment. Vision Life Ministries fulfills the mission of Jesus to heal the brokenhearted, bring freedom to the captives, and set at liberty those who have experienced oppression. The Freedom and Fullness seminar lays a strong Biblical foundation for deliverance and inner healing, charts the path to freedom for every participant and provides an opportunity for ministry within a group setting. Throughout the day and a half seminar, men, women and young people experience a power encounter with God that leads to freedom and wholeness.

The seminar helps you to discover the answers to these and many other questions:

- Why do I struggle with the same problems again and again?
- Why are there barriers I can't get over?
- What are these negative patterns I see in my family line?
- How can I get over this anger I feel all the time?
- Can I truly be healed from the hurts in my life?
- Is it possible to really let go of the past?
- What are strongholds and how do they develop?
- Why do I do the very things I have said I'd never do?

The freedom and fullness seminar is a prerequisite to all of the vision life ministries training courses.

Freedom and Fullness Seminar also available on DVD or audio CD.

NEXT STEP SEMINAR

Reach Your Destiny One Choice at a Time

This one-day seminar gives participants the understanding to destroy self-defeating attitudes and behaviors and walk forward on their journey. It will benefit believers at all levels of maturity as well as those who need additional help in learning to walk in freedom. The goal of Next Step is that each person who attends will have a better understanding of their root issues and the factors which affect their spiritual development and be able to leave the seminar with an "action plan" to expedite their freedom and growth. The seminar consists of teaching, application activities and ministry.

Learn how to . . .

+ Take responsibility for your own life.
+ Cultivate your ongoing walk with God.
+ Learn to cooperate with the Holy Spirit.
+ Trace actions and reaction to root causes.
+ Discern the lies of the enemy that keep you from your purpose.
+ Replace the negative thought patterns that sabotage you.
+ Have more fulfilling relationships with others.
+ Establish new patterns of behavior.
+ Break "trigger points."
+ Receive prayer ministry for areas of need.
+ Make an action plan for continued change.
+ Much more!

Next Step Seminar now available only on audio CDs with manual.

PERSONAL MINISTRY TRAINING

Personal Ministry Training will take the individual to the next level. It will encourage, train and equip those who desire wholeness in their own lives and/or desire to extend the Kingdom of God through ministering deliverance and inner healing. After participating in this three-part training school, a person will be prepared to lead personal ministry sessions. Each training is a Thursday night, Friday and Saturday.

Personal Ministry Training One

Personal Ministry Training One develops the strategy of the warrior and focuses on training for leading personal ministry sessions.

Some of the major subjects covered are . . .

+ Scriptural basis for deliverance
+ Authority of the believer
+ 2-5-14 strategy for deliverance
+ Healing the brokenhearted
+ Weapons of our warfare
+ Learning to listen
+ How to interview
+ The ongoing nature of deliverance
+ Actual demonstration of a deliverance session using the 2-5-14 strategy

Personal Ministry Training Two

Personal Ministry Training Two develops the heart of the warrior and focuses on the attitudes and character necessary to be fruitful and effective in life and ministry.

Some of the subjects covered are . . .

+ Shattering the foundation of rebellion
+ Dealing with mother/father wounds
+ Changing the cause of prolonged pain
+ Removing shame
+ Recovering identity
+ Disconnecting from witchcraft
+ Overcoming codependency
+ Developing a pure heart
+ Anointing of the warrior
+ Confidentiality
+ Sexual integrity and much more

PERSONAL MINISTRY TRAINING THREE

Personal Ministry Training Three develops the gifts and skills of the warrior. It focuses on demonstration and participation in actual personal deliverance sessions. During the course of these two and one-half days, the students will be engaged in actual full deliverance sessions using the 2-5-14 strategy of deliverance and inner healing.

This hands-on involvement in the exercising of their discerning abilities, testing of their spiritual authority, utilizing their listening and interview skills and increasing of their anointing completes the three-part training school. A person will be prepared to lead personal ministry sessions upon completion of the Personal Ministry Training.

SPECIALIZED TRAININGS

Now Available on Audio CD

Learning To Recognize Those Who Are DID/SRA

Redeeming The Next Generation: How To Minister
Deliverance And Healing To Children

Cleansing Your House And Land From Spiritual Darkness

Advanced Inner Healing

ORDER FORM

■ Call to place your order: **(469) 549-0730**   ■ Fax your order: **(469) 549-0736**
■ Postal orders: **Vision Life Ministries, P.O. Box 153691, Irving, TX 75015**
■ Order online: **www.visionlife.org**

Title	Price		Quantity		Amount
Islam Unmasked	$10	x	_____	=	_____
Portals to Cleansing	$12	x	_____	=	_____
Portals to Cleansing Kit	$12	x	_____	=	_____
Shadow Boxing	$13	x	_____	=	_____
Boxeando Con La Sombra	$12	x	_____	=	_____
Shame	$13	x	_____	=	_____

Shipping and Handling _____
(Please add $6 for the first book and $2 for each additional book)

Total _____

_____ Please send more information about Freedom and Fullness seminars

_____ Please send more information about Personal Ministry Training

_____
Name (please print clearly)

_____
Address   Apt.

_____
City   State   Zip

_____
Country   Phone

_____
E-mail

Method of Payment

____ Check/Money Order (payable to Vision Life Ministries)   ____ Visa   ____ MasterCard

_____
Card Number   Expiration Date

_____
Card Holder (please print clearly)

_____
Signature

ORDER FORM

■ Call to place your order: **(469) 549-0730** ■ Fax your order: **(469) 549-0736**
■ Postal orders: **Vision Life Ministries, P.O. Box 153691, Irving, TX 75015**
■ Order online: **www.visionlife.org**

Title	Price	Quantity	Amount
Islam Unmasked	$10	x _____	= _____
Portals to Cleansing	$12	x _____	= _____
Portals to Cleansing Kit	$12	x _____	= _____
Shadow Boxing	$13	x _____	= _____
Boxeando Con La Sombra	$12	x _____	= _____
Shame	$13	x _____	= _____

Shipping and Handling _____
(Please add $6 for the first book and $2 for each additional book)

Total _____

_____ Please send more information about Freedom and Fullness seminars

_____ Please send more information about Personal Ministry Training

_____
Name (please print clearly)

_____
Address   Apt.

_____
City   State   Zip

_____
Country   Phone

_____
E-mail

Method of Payment

___ Check/Money Order (payable to Vision Life Ministries)   ___ Visa ___ MasterCard

_____
Card Number   Expiration Date

_____
Card Holder (please print clearly)

_____
Signature